10 Truths About Leadership
...it's not just about winning

Pete Luongo

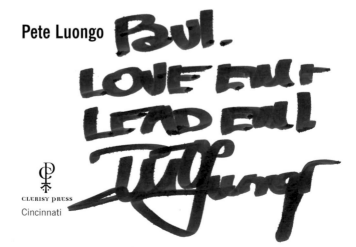

CLERISY PRESS
Cincinnati

Library of Congress Cataloging-in-Publication Data

Luongo, Pete 1934–
    10 truths about leadership : it's not just about winning /
      by Pete Luongo.
      p. cm.
      ISBN-13: 978-1-57860-302-2 (alk. paper)
      ISBN-10: 1-57860-302-1 (alk. paper)
      1. Leadership. 2. Respect for persons 3. Integrity.
    4. Performance standards. 5. Employee empowerment.
    I. Title. II. Title: Ten truths about leadership.

      HD57.7L865 2007
      658.4'092—dc22
      2007013384

For further information, contact the publisher:

CLERISY PRESS
P.O. BOX 8874
CINCINNATI, OHIO 45208-0874

Edited by Richard Hunt
Cover and interior designed by Angela Wilcox
Distributed by Publishers Group West
First edition, fourth printing 2010

PRINTED in China

Dedication

To the University of Dayton: its scholars, professors, administration, and especially the priests and brothers of the Society of Mary. It was during those formative years as a student that I learned we are ultimately judged by our willingness to make a difference in other peoples' lives. Upon retirement I've returned to this wonderful university, working with numerous groups and boards. It is my hope that I can extend to others the same chance to succeed. It's a very special time in my life and I'm grateful for the opportunity to give back to such an extraordinary place, and help perpetuate our university's mission of learn, lead, and serve.

Acknowledgments

I would like to offer my heartfelt thanks to the following people for their encouragement and support as I was writing this book, as well as their positive influence in all phases of my life. Remarkably, through the artistic talents of Richard Launius, the likenesses of a few of these special people grace the pages of this book.

Dan Graham (appearing on pages 7, 67, and 81), eighth president of The Berry Company. His character, commitment, and competitiveness made him special.

Kathy-Geiger Schwab (appearing on pages 7 and 67), executive vice president of The Berry Company. Her counsel and insights were invaluable.

Debbie Luongo (appearing on pages 21 and 67), my wife of 38 years. Her love, support, and encouragement have allowed me to pursue my dreams.

Jerry Cheadle (appearing on pages 41 and 67), group

president, AT&T Yellow Pages. A caring leader whose capacity to grow a business enriched me.

Richard Launius (appearing on page 53), vice president, systems, AT&T. A great caricaturist who unselfishly gave of his time to provide the illustrations for this book.

Peter and Matt Luongo (appearing on page 99). Our sons have given us an enormous sense of pride as Debbie and I have watched them grow into outstanding young men.

Elmer Smith (appearing on page 157), retired president of The Berry Company. If not for his friendship and support for more than 33 years, I would not have written this book.

To John Snyder, Mark Lane, Anita Moore, Bill Ferguson, Randolph Melichar, Greg Meineke and so many others who allowed me to be part of their lives; they've become an enormous source of pride as I've watched them grow personally and professionally.

To Ray Eshelman, Tom Murphy, Paul Resinger, Larry

Taylor, Bill Tripp and Don Perozzi who provided wonderful role models as bosses as my career progressed.

To the Berrys—L.M., John Sr., and John Jr.—for creating a company that helped so many of us live out our dreams.

To the Carroll High School athletes, including Pat Sullivan, Lou Renzi, and Mike Hennessy, and the rest of our team who made a commitment to a sport in which they had never before competed, yet in just three years became accomplished wrestlers. This team helped me recognize the magic of leadership in terms of influencing others' lives.

To Doug Myers, Jerry DiPippo and many other business partners who taught me that loyalty and respect for one's relationships always takes precedent over self-interest.

To Dan Curran, Clay Mathile, Marc Levy, JP Nausef, Doug Franklin, John Nowak, Dennis Rediker and a host of others for their unselfishness as they have devoted themselves to making our region a better place to live.

To Jack Schrader, Don Zimmer, Gary McCans and Charley Mazza whose life-time friendships have always been a source of encouragement and inspiration.

Special thanks to Marty Grunder who convinced me to write this book when others failed.

To Richard Launius, for his unselfishness and creativity in providing the art for this book.

Finally, thanks to my publisher Richard Hunt. He helped me realize my dream of telling this story.

Foreword

by Curt W. Coffman, Co-Author of the *New York Times* bestselling *First, Break all the Rules*

Let me be frank *(and I don't mean Sinatra)*, I am nothing short of being bored and exhausted with the thousands of leadership books that have come to swim in the pools of bookstores everywhere. Leadership is one of those topics that people love to hear themselves **talk about** but very few choose to **listen to**. We all have a **theory** that has largely been formed from our own justification of why we did or continue to do certain things. Books, articles and papers from academics to alleged renaissance leaders have produced pontifications about how to **be** a great leader.

I am amazed at the tremendous amount of creativity put into the discovery of a new model or a new set of metaphors while the actual meat of the book takes a back seat. Many of these books have become reference guides for me to find both pithy and slightly off-center ways of saying the same thing. Try it—it works!

While my cynicism is obvious, I find it refreshing when a text comes along that brings back those moments of a-ha's and genuine intellectual and emotional engagement. I really live for those words that come off the page, strumming a chord of curiosity and providing a moment of new understanding. So has the book I'm proud to introduce to you.

Pete Luongo didn't decide to sit down and write a book on leadership; he was called to do so. See, there are those times in one's life where the ability to "not" do something is no longer an alternative. Pete and his witty, charismatic and "loving" personality are mere byproducts of a set of experiences he has noted, been moved by, and found enormous success with. There is no doubt in my mind that this book began long before Pete was writing it.

This may sound strange, but this is a book that has long been in process and only recently found its author. Now, don't get me wrong. Pete is one of the most "full of life" and passionate people I know, and his life experiences are a perfect fit for this book's longing to be told and understood. His experiences simply became the medium for which a set of truisms are told.

In reading Pete's text, I am convinced that these truths should be incorporated into the business and personal lives of leaders, managers, and people following their passions everywhere. This set of truths will not bring about an academic revolution in the field of leadership and management, but they will lead us back to the basic and most critical issues that determine our impact and success.

See, this is not a leadership book at all! It is a time-tested, proven course illuminating the golden thread connecting every person to a life of excellence and purpose.

Table of Contents

Introduction

Okay, I admit it. When I retired as president and CEO of The Berry Company, writing a book wasn't at the top of my list of priorities. But whenever I spoke to groups about leadership and organizational efficiency, the feedback I received, overwhelmingly, was people wanted a book that captured the experiences and insights I had just shared with them.

Most business and personal improvement books seem to fall into one of two categories. The first group is based on well-documented, exhaustive research that morphs into complex solutions and theories. The second group relies on a stimulating call to action, that is, the "rah" in rah-rah.

Unfortunately, too few focus in on the most difficult challenge for us all, as individuals and organizations—**How do we value our lives?** My vision with this book is to inform and excite. My belief is that, beneath the spreadsheets, strategies and psychological tests, the truths really are pretty straightforward. What I will share with you is a simple, but not over-simplified, understanding of the values shared by those who thrive in business as well as in life.

Becoming a leader can be daunting; at the same time, it's a

hugely rewarding endeavor. Finding an opportunity to lead, as well as finding in yourself the courage and clarity to lead others, is central to our existence. Sometimes the situation can be thrust upon you, other times it is a position that takes decades of hard work and commitment to achieve. Coaches for youth sports teams, executive vice-presidents and CEOs, community board members, PTA and PTO volunteers, individuals running small businesses and those running divisions of massive corporations—there are leaders needed in every stripe of life.

Look around you—leaders abound. Look in the mirror—that same right stuff is also inside of you.

This book is about the ten truths leaders understand will lead to success, time and again. This book is also about a personal journey that taught me that our lives, ultimately, will be judged by our ability and willingness to make a difference in other people's lives. As a business leader, corporate strategist, CEO, board chair, college professor, high school wrestling coach, high school and collegiate wrestling official, husband, father, lecturer, leader, and a friend, I recognized (finally at the age of thirty-seven!) a code of conduct must be a part of everything we say, do, and ask of ourselves and others.

Many leaders remember that life-changing moment when, almost suddenly, it became crystal clear what must be done and committed to that end. It wasn't until I was faced with that one epiphany in life, which requires each of us to rebalance life's priorities and brings a new understanding to what we already know, that I recognized all we do must be the result of a set of mores: a required set of behaviors appropriate for the circumstance we are attempting to influence. By accepting that all of our actions must be measured by specific, well-defined behaviors, I was able to build a model that was both sustainable in terms of results and yet allowed people to retain their personal dignity as they pursued their life's plan.

At the Berry Company in 1994, we formally implemented "The Leadership Pledge," an operating philosophy that was built on a set of behaviors. This established a foundation that focused our efforts on recruiting talented performers, providing them the tools to do their job, defining expectations, providing meaningful feedback and holding each member of the organization accountable for all of their actions.

Achieving success, however you define it, is ultimately about knowing and executing those behaviors that are tied to what's most important to you and your organization.

Effective leaders understand the need for discipline and focus on THOSE BEHAVIORS that drive results, rather

than focusing only on the results. Master THESE ACTIONS and you'll achieve the results. Focus only on the results, and it's very likely you'll lose your way.

That's what happened to me.

While so many of my examples are drawn from the business world, I assure you the tenets, obstacles, and truths detailed on these pages apply to every facet of life. Many times, it's easier to make a point about something learned at work since that part of our lives is so clearly black and white. But these principles carry value in every situation, from being a parent to being a coach to being a friend. It's not surprising that the data backing up these findings emerged from the business sector because companies are great at keeping score, adding things up and measuring results. As executive director of the University of Dayton's Center for Leadership and Executive Development (one of the many wonderful experiences I've enjoyed since retirement), I've had the privilege of working with some of the world's most famous thought leaders on issues including leadership, change, strategy, and growth. What I've heard from the likes of Bob Quinn, Curt Coffman, Robert Cooper, Daniel Kim, Charles Dwyer, James Lucas, John Maxwell, Jim Kouzes, Ram Charan, Jeffery Pfeffer, Jim Loehr, and numerous others have inspired me to share this model with you. Rare is the person who can understand the theories and principles and still excite the practitioners, "the soldiers in the field," who make success happen. This book does precisely that by addressing all aspects of our lives. I'm extremely proud to share with you that in every case, the data backs up what my intuition was telling me all along. **These truths are simple. Acknowledging and abiding by them takes some work. Trust yourself.**

CHAPTER ONE

Leaders
Care
but Never
Compromise

When any organization is operating at its best, it's not because of technological superiority, competitive strategies, or product differentiation. Certainly those factors are important, but an organization achieves maximum efficiency through people, relationships, and love—love for ourselves, love for each other, and love for what we do every day.

"Love" is not a word lightly tossed around corporate America. In fact, I would suggest it's the most underutilized and most misunderstood word in business.

As you'll soon see, when I brought love into my business vocabulary, it had a dramatic impact on my life. We will use this word many times throughout the book, so let's examine a few of love's distinctions.

The first is defining love in a business context. Love of the self at the professional level is simply about faith in who we are and confidence as we approach our life each and every day. Next, love for others is about trust and mutual respect for one another. Love at the professional level is a love for what we do every day and is simply about our passion.

The second distinction is that it's not an unconditional love without responsibility. It must be conditional love with consequences

attached—this is called tough love. It's a paradox. This is an enormous challenge for everyone involved. Unconditional love is at the core of our marriage vows. It's also the bond between parent and child.

This same tacit agreement requires honest feedback. Without honest feedback, there are serious limitations on our ability as leaders, coaches, parents, and friends. For without this level of truth, we don't allow our employees, our athletes, our children, and our friends to develop to their full potential. Far too often, we justify our lack of candor as an excuse for not wanting to cause anger, pain, and resentment, but in reality we are doing more damage than good.

On more than one occasion, I found myself in the emotionally challenging position of telling employees at The Berry Company, "I love you, but you just don't get to work here anymore." As difficult as that message was to deliver, they were better off working elsewhere because they were in circumstances where they just weren't going to prosper.

The third, and last, distinction is that blending strength of character and love for your fellow man does not weaken your manhood or womanhood. Blending character and love is a fundamental quality for leaders, one that I underline with audiences because it's so important. I have seen far too many leaders who are afraid to show the side that makes them special.

Dr. Robert Quinn, from the University of Michigan, and

one of the thought leaders who has spoken at the Center for Leadership & Executive Development, spotlights the best leaders as "transformative" and defines them as "those who are enormously demanding and enormously caring." I've worked with countless business leaders, and very few have a problem with the demand side of the model...that's easy! It's the caring side of the model that causes most leaders to struggle.

Caring defines our uniqueness not only as leaders but as human beings. Daniel Goleman's book *Emotional Intelligence* was a major breakthrough and much has been written to support his belief that to be effective in getting the most from people around you, they've got to know you care. Very few of us are comfortable enough with ourselves to reach that breakthrough in relationships. Paradoxically, far too often we are guilty of over-managing the relationship which takes away the responsibility of people managing themselves. The most effective leaders, as Quinn noted, learn to master both sides.

As we prepared to roll out "The Leadership Pledge" as the company's operating philosophy, we spent a great deal of time uncovering the defining moments in our lives and what they really felt like. Think back to a euphoric experience when you stretched yourself beyond your capacity or you dared to dream big, either individually or as an organization.

I describe that feeling as "arriving at the destination." Others call it winning, or getting to the top of the mountain.

While winning has to be the ultimate objective for any individual or organization because it's how we are measured, there is a vast distinction between outcome goals (the final destination) and process goals (the journey to get there).

Outcome goals are those milestones that we tend to affix a number—a sales goal, a revenue target, or the ten pounds we want to lose. If I've learned nothing else over forty years of coaching, leading and advising, I realize it is paramount to prevent these outcome goals from shaping how we feel about ourselves.

Process goals are those objectives we put in place to reach our outcome goals. These must be seen as links in the chain, and in many ways, are the ultimate reason for success or failure.

First and foremost, we must have big dreams if we are going to get the most from our lives. Far too many people underestimate themselves. Only when we truly dare to stretch ourselves beyond our capacity, to dream big, can we get a glimpse of how far we can go. Once we see our goal in our mind's eye, it becomes real, attainable, and reachable.

So the question is . . . where do we get the daily shot of "I can do this"? I believe we get it from the pursuit of those big dreams. That's the source of our self-esteem. We can't base our sense of self-worth solely on outcomes, and it's not other people's responsibility to make us feel good about ourselves. If we behave in the way we know will yield positive results, our self-esteem is reinforced, and our actions echo our intentions.

I'm almost left speechless when I hear that often-used comment following the passing of a family member or friend, "It makes you think about your priorities." My response is always the same: "Since no one leaves this earth alive, why does it take someone's passing to re-evaluate our priorities?"

It's quite simple: Yesterday is history, tomorrow is a mystery, and today is a gift. For me, it's always been about the hunt, not the kill. Vince Lombardi invoked the same when he talked about his '68 Packers. He said, "We're going to chase the hell out of perfection, and hopefully we'll catch some excellence along the way." In the end, our lives are about the journey we all take!

There are two friends who accompany everyone on the journey to achieving success and becoming a leader: change and choice. There are two things we know about change. First, change is constant in our lives—you can't get away from it, yet folks struggle mightily to stop it. Second, change never leaves us like it found us!

As it relates to the journey, I want to draw the distinction between incremental change and "deep change" as Dr. Robert E. Quinn describes in his book of the same name. He says, "Incremental change usually does not disrupt past patterns . . . [and] is an extension of the past. Deep change differs from incremental change in that it requires new ways of thinking and behaving. It represents a change that is major in scope, discontinuous with the past and generally irreversible. Deep change means surrendering control."

So you need to make choices when confronted with inevitable change. Quinn goes on to say, "There is an important link between deep change at the personal level and deep change at the organizational level. To make deep personal change is to develop a new paradigm, one that is more effective with today's realities."

Every day our lives are different due to internal change or change that is externally imposed on us. For instance, externally, our lives have been forever altered since 9/11. Internally, I've watched too many friends stricken with cancer and have marveled at the choices they made in how to confront it. Most of what happens to us in our lives depends on how we choose to respond and what choices we make when confronted with change.

It was in Buffalo, New York, in July of 1981 that I, along with several colleagues at The Berry Company, made the choice to find a better way . . . and our lives, personally and professionally, were forever changed for the better. This is the journey I want to share with you.

In the yellow page industry, we manage our business by annual schedules and deadlines called campaigns. All customers had to be contacted and all agreements signed.

14

Advertising had to be designed and ready for the printer in accordance with schedules and deadlines. The New York division, which I managed, had just completed the Buffalo campaign. This unit had been in a downward spiral, and as the campaign ended, we hit rock bottom. There were lots of contributing factors. The economy in Buffalo was devastated as the steel industry collapsed. Unemployment reached staggering numbers and we had serious competition from the White Directory Company, which meant that for the first time, advertisers had a choice for how they spent their advertising dollars.

Internally, we were struggling as well. We had lost a number of our salespeople and managers to our competitor, and the usual morale issues that afflict an organization in disarray were mounting. The company we worked for, New York Telephone, was terribly insensitive to the plight of the advertiser as well as our ability to meet unreasonable goals.

Only many years later can I look back on this life-altering experience and realize it's never the economy nor the competition that brings an organization down, but rather the inability to respond. That response has to start with the leader.

As division manager I was focused on three things back then: winning (which was important to me then and still is, by the way), getting ahead (or maybe a better description, climbing that corporate ladder), and pleasing my boss (preserving our culture). While all of those elements are necessary to

success, I was missing the key element. What I didn't understand, realize, or appreciate was that I was imposing my value
system on a hundred and seven employees with little regard
for what they believed was important to them.

So when they looked to me for leadership, what they
got instead was a leader facing failure for the first time in his
business career and behaving accordingly. I wasn't winning. I
was losing . . . and in a big way. I got my first life lesson about
leadership:

The only time we realize our dreams

is when we help others realize theirs.

One of the many things that makes The Berry Company
an extraordinary place to work is the commitment to dialogue
between senior management and all of our employees. At
about the time the division was unraveling in Buffalo, the company was conducting our annual employee survey. As you can
imagine, given these circumstances, when the scores got to
human resources at headquarters in Dayton, red lights went
off and the sirens blared. There was a crisis in Buffalo! As you
might expect, human resources responded like the Kemper
Calvary, and the feedback sessions were quite ugly.

On the heels of the report, I got the dreaded call to come to the home office. I made the trip fearing the worst. Would it be a transfer, a demotion, or the pink slip? Much to my surprise, it was none of the above. Enter life lesson number two: **The people who care about us the most are those who stand shoulder to shoulder with us during our most difficult times.**

At the time, I worked for Tom Murphy, the regional manager in Rochester, and John Berry Jr., the vice president of the east region and the grandson of the company's founder.

They were both consistent in their opinion that while I was relentless in pursuit of results, I had created an environment in which our employees felt under-appreciated and disrespected. In short, I was hurting the people I cared about the most!

This devastated me. The good news was both John and Tom offered their support and confidence and they allowed me to be the one who fixed the problem. I went back to Buffalo, humbled but determined to earn back the trust and loyalty of my colleagues.

Upon return, I did something I had never done before. I stood in front of all one hundred and seven people, with a deep sense of contrition, and said I was sorry. There were a lot of tears in that room, mostly mine. I promised them that while we were still expected to make sales quotas and meet New

York Telephone's expectations, it would never be at the expense of each other's dignity.

Solving life's problems is a two-part process. First, you must realize you've got a problem. Second, you've got to figure out how to correct it. While the problem was obvious, the solution was not.

Bill Tripp, our vice president of HR and a mentor to me, suggested that I spend some time at the Center for Values Research in Dallas. The Berry Company had employed CVR as consultants to administer our attitude surveys and consult on other HR issues.

Central to my journey were Vince Flowers and Charley Hughes, partners at the Center. Both of them were heavily influenced in their practice by Dr. Clare Graves, a renowned psychologist who had done extensive research in the 1950s, '60s, and '70s on value systems.

So I spent a week with them in Dallas. The short version of what they said to me was

I needed to go back to Buffalo and create a behavior-driven organization rather than a sales-driven one.

When I arrived back in Buffalo, I gathered all my managers in my office on a Sunday night and told them I've been to the mountain and found the solution. That is how our leadership journey began in earnest.

CHAPTER TWO

Leaders Know
the Value of Good
People

When we began our journey, we asked ourselves the first critical question: "If we're serious about finding a better way, where do we start?"

Leaders know the one constant in business and life is people. It's ludicrous that people can too often be ignored or overlooked. How can achieving success in every organization not focus on its most critical asset—its people?

Whether an organization succeeds or fails is determined by the people who show up for work every day. It is the people with whom the customers interact who make a difference. In fact, when your company's name is mentioned, it is the faces and

performances of your people that your customers remember.

To help us with our business transformation, we hearkened back to our founder, Mr. L.M. Berry, a truly extraordinary man. L.M. came to Dayton in 1910 and started selling advertising on the back of train schedules. Eventually, he approached Dayton Home Telephone Company and offered to sell advertising in their phone number guides to help defray the cost of printing. It was this concept that led L.M. Berry to become one of the first creators of the yellow pages concept as we know it today.

Back in the '30s and '40s, Mr. Berry traveled the country by train, relentlessly calling up more telephone companies to sign up their yellow page directory business. By the late '50s, L.M. Berry and Company had become the country's largest independent yellow page advertising agency in the United States.

I was blessed with the opportunity to know L.M. for the last ten years of his life, and I heard him say many times that he named his company L.M. Berry and Company because he was L.M. Berry, but more importantly, **his people were his company**. Although the name was changed to The Berry Company in 1992 to become more contemporary, his belief that our people represent our primary asset continues to serve as its guiding principle.

There is a valuable lesson here for all of us. **When you feel you or your company has veered off course or is searching for new identity, think back to your, or the company's, original intentions, which tend to be straightforward, focused, and strong.** Businesses can drift away from these benchmarks as the years go by.

It's not easy for many organizations to weave together the past, the present, and the future. Kathy Geiger-Schwab, the current executive vice president for The Berry Company, created a phrase that became part of our everyday business vocabulary: **"Old Values, New Ideas."** "Old Values" represented the culture that defined The Berry Company's legacy, reminding us how critical it was that we retain what made us unique by recognizing that we could not create the future by recreating the past. "New Ideas" represented the go-forward strategy based upon creativity, imagination, ingenuity and courage. I believe that this balance must be reached if organizations are going to be competitive going forward regardless of their pursuit.

It is of utmost importance, both in today's global economy as well as our local communities, to find talented performers. Although much has been written about the need for hiring quality employees, it's obvious that much is lost in execution. During the last several years, I have been associated with over a hundred different organizations, and I'm shocked at the lack of emphasis on recruiting, hiring, finding, and keeping good people. I'm even more surprised at the lack of participation of senior management in this most critical function. **Finding and keeping good people must be the number one priority for all organizations!**

Not long ago, I had the opportunity to address a large group of human resource senior executives. I asked the audience, "How much time do you spend in the recruiting phase of your job?" Their responses both surprised and disappointed me. By their own admission, they spend most of their HR time getting non-productive, disgruntled employees out of their respective organizations. As the dismissal process becomes more complex, messy, and costly, the solution is clear: Why not spend more time up front on selecting the right employees?

In 2006, we surveyed the more than fifteen hundred executives who attended the Center for Leadership & Executive Development programs over the previous six years. They said their number one concern in the upcoming year was the hiring and retention of talent. Your strategic and operational priorities must center on getting the best people to work with you. If this isn't senior management's primary goal, then the company will falter and personnel will not be a priority for the rest of the organization. As president/CEO of The Berry Company, I spent at least thirty percent of my time involved in selection and retention strategies and personnel engagement.

Finding and keeping good people must be a personal priority for every individual in the organization.

I once asked a large group of first- and second-level sales managers at The Berry Company how many of them had personally recruited a salesperson, just one, over the last twelve months. The question produced a paltry twenty-five percent show of hands. The truth is, even in companies where hiring and retaining good people is the number one priority, this focus can still slip away in the hectic pace of business if it is not constantly reinforced.

I've never been opposed to college recruiting, job fairs, online recruiting, newspaper ads, and so on. While I support these resources as part of a recruiting strategy, too often they are the painful result of not effectively engaging your employees in the recruiting and selection process.

Your best employees are your best recruiters. Why? First, who knows the job and what's required to be successful better than your best people?

Second, "winners run around with winners!" With high levels of employee engagement, you will increase your odds of attracting those prospective employees who are experiencing success in their own careers but weren't aware of the wonderful opportunities awaiting them at your company. I always loved to disrupt people's lives by making them aware of what they were missing by not being at Berry!

To quote Aristotle, "We are what we repeatedly do. Excellence, then, is not an act, but a habit."

OBSTACLE 1 Poor Selection

As the journey began, we ran into our first obstacle in addressing our first priority, people. We were guilty of poor selection. We had developed two bad habits that impeded our efforts to re-build the division. The first is something I call "the body count." Under the pressure to get the work done on time, we would forsake all we knew about making quality hires and simply hire "bodies."

In the yellow pages world, the only thing as important as meeting our advertisers' and telephone customer's revenue expectations is getting the directories published and distributed on time. We backed into our sales schedule by determining market penetration, productivity standards, and the number of salespeople required to meet those publication dates. Even though we didn't have the sophisticated assessment tools available today, we had the ability to hire those who offered the most potential . . . when we were patient.

Every business has its own deadlines and commitments. You know yours and probably feel that same pressure when facing a crucial deadline to make certain you have someone in place to get everything done. You seek someone with "experience and a proven track record." As the dates grow closer and that position remains unfilled, the criteria for candidates becomes "experience preferred . . . but not necessary." Soon it becomes "just need a warm body." This is a recipe for eventual disaster. Deadlines have a funny way of warping our vision.

The second problem is what I describe as the "You haven't worked for me yet" syndrome. Back then, I thought we could change people. I would even sign off on hiring direct descendants of Charles Manson and say it's going to be okay because they haven't worked for me yet!

Of the hundreds of case studies, business publications, journals, and articles I've been exposed to, none is more appropriate in supporting our first truth than the work done by Marcus Buckingham and Curt Coffman at Gallup and published in their best seller *First, Break All the Rules*. In their chapter "The Decade of the Brain," they confront this most important issue of attempting to change people:

> How much of you can be changed? If you hate meeting people can you learn to love icebreaking with strangers? If you shy away from confrontation, can you be made to revel in

the cut and thrust of debate? If the bright lights make you sweat can you be taught to thrill to the challenge of public speaking? Can you carve new talents?

Many managers and many companies assume that the answer to all of these questions is "Yes." With the best of intentions, they tell their employees that everyone has the same potential. They encourage employees to be open and dedicated to learning new ways to behave. To help them climb up the company hierarchy, they send their employees to training classes designated to teach all manners of new behaviors—empathy, assertiveness, relationship building, innovations, strategic thinking. From their perspective, one of the most admirable qualities an employee can possess is the willingness to transform themselves through learning and self-discipline. This couldn't be further from the truth.

The world's great managers according to Gallup share quite a different approach, which leads to this mantra:

"People don't change much.

Don't waste your time trying to put in what was left out.

Try to draw out what was left in.

That is hard enough."

The research was compiled by Gallup from interviews with eighty thousand managers. It validates what we learned in 1981, both intuitively and out of necessity, and has become the single most important lesson any parent, leader, coach, or friend can ever grasp: I can make you more than you are, I just can't make you something you're not!

Poor selection is far too often associated with managers and leaders spending precious time trying to change others and not recognizing that

People don't change!

More importantly, even if they could, we don't have the time or skill to change them.

What are the qualities and attributes that our very best people possess? What is the common thread running through all of our talent? A few years ago, I read this line: "It ain't about who you are or what you are, it's about what you do with what you've got." I disagreed with that quote then, and still do, because it is about who you are! The "who you are" is another way to say "character." And it only makes sense that every hiring decision has got to start with character.

Webster's Dictionary defines character as, "possessing those attributes of ethics, integrity, and morality that distinguish one individual from another."

Dr. Martin Luther King Jr. said, "I have a dream that my four little children will one day live in a nation where they will not be judged by the color of their skin but by the content of their character." Although he was speaking primarily to spotlight racial issues, the baseline is the same: character.

When I teach the NCAA-required Life Skills course for freshmen athletes at the University of Dayton, I constantly remind the students to be more concerned with their character than with their reputations. **Character is what you really are. Your reputation is what people think you are.**

I'm quite often asked the question:

Can I change my character? My answer is—we certainly can improve it because we own it. It is who we are and we influence it every day by all of our actions. It represents everything we think, everything we say, and everything we do!

Every hiring decision must start with character and it's not negotiable.

What you do with what you've got is about "talent." Talent, according to Buckingham and Coffman defines the "why" and the "how" of a person. They go on to say, "Your own skills and knowledge are relatively easy to identify. You had to acquire them, and therefore they are apart and distinct. They are 'Not you.' But your talents? **Your talents are simply your recurring patterns of behavior. They are your very essence and they are the "what."** It takes a rare objectivity to be able to stand back from yourself and pick the unique patterns that make you You!"

The next question that had to be answered as we rebuilt our sales force was: What were the attributes, qualities and behaviors of our most talented employees?

The first attribute is competitiveness. It was an absolute requirement in our selection and hiring. I could make a strong case for organizations requiring people with a competitive spirit, in most positions. While being competitive is often associated with athletics and testosterone, I've found it in academics, business, and a myriad of other circumstances where there was recognition, a prize, or profit associated with the results.

One of my greatest surprises and proudest moments as a parent came when both of our sons were members of the John Carroll Catholic High School Concert Choir in Birmingham, Alabama. Though both boys were athletes, each would tell you unequivocally that the greatest coach they had in high school was Ken Berg, the choir director. The competition in and around that experience was intense, from tryouts to international competition. Not only did they learn how to make beautiful music, they learned what it was like to compete and win in the most beautiful of circumstances.

The person you hire need not be an athlete or have played competitive sports. However, it's crucial they have some background of competition or some evidence that the person you're hiring understands what it means to be competitive.

The second critical attribute is commitment. *Webster's* definition of commitment is "the act of pledging oneself to a particular position or the state of being bound emotionally or intellectually to something." Unless an individual has been bound to something and has been involved from beginning to end, there is little chance that commitment can be otherwise taught.

Passion is the third attribute and is absolutely mandatory. I believe it is the differentiator between those who do and those who don't. When I was a high school wrestling coach, the sign in our wrestling room simply stated, "Passion is the combination of talent plus heart."

Capacity to learn is a critical attribute for every leader, and leader-to-be. The ability to learn and expand in order to meet the needs of the rapidly changing world has never been more important than it is today.

If character, competitiveness, commitment, passion, and

the capacity to learn are not present, well, as the great Italian philosopher Joe Pesci, said in *Goodfellas*, "Forget about it!"

Past Performance Predicts Future Behavior

It's simple! Find people whose talents align properly with the requirements of the position so there will be a high probability of them being successful. If they've been successful in the past, it's likely they'll be successful in the future.

I had a professor in college, George Beirsack, who gave me a great piece of advice that has stayed with me my entire life. He said, "Son, if you're fortunate enough to find something you love doing, consider yourself in the minority. And, if they are willing to pay you for it that makes it even better."

Several years ago, I spoke to roughly three hundred dealers for Aamco Transmissions. I shared the program with psychologist and author, Dr. Joe Currier. Afterward, he asked me, "How can someone come into your business with a high probability of being successful, yet never make it?" My response to Joe was that he was more qualified to answer than me. You see, I don't know of an assessment tool that measures someone's heart. **If you don't love what you do, you just won't be very good at it.**

Past performance predicts future behavior. You've got to find your sweet spot and your strengths. The best example I can share with you is the hiring of Dan Graham as a sales rep in 1978. The first time I met Dan Graham, I was officiating a high school wrestling match, and Dan was wrestling for Alter High School in Kettering, Ohio. Over the next two years, I had plenty of opportunities to get to know Dan, both as an excellent wrestler and also as an outstanding young man. What I knew, even then, was that Dan had heart.

Dan went on to Heidleberg College where he played football and wrestled. While Dan possessed natural leadership skills, nothing was more convincing to me than when he suffered a career-ending knee injury. Amazingly, he remained the same committed young man, but he focused his energy in new directions without letting adversity destroy his future. It was his character, competitiveness, commitment, passion, and capacity to grow that gave Dan a high probability of being successful in our business.

After graduation from college, Dan came to see me. I hired him the following week, and twenty-five years later, he became only the eighth president of The Berry Company in 93 years.

Discoveries

1 First and foremost, selecting and retaining quality people must be the highest priority of every organization. It takes resources and commitment to find and keep the right people, and the commitment to do so must start at the top. My advice to senior executives/leadership is simple: If it's important to you, it will be important to everyone on the team. Engagement of all employees is a must.

2 Recognize that fundamental changes in people have to come from within themselves. We can't change who they are, but we can influence their behavior by being crystal clear in communicating what we are asking them to do and asking them who to be.

3 We must constantly remind ourselves as leaders, coaches, parents and friends that we can make someone more than they are but we cannot make them something they're not.

CHAPTER THREE

Leaders Inspire Rather than Motivate

T he subject of motivation triggers countless debates in leadership, management, and coaching circles. Whose responsibility is it to motivate? Do we own that responsibility individually or does it belong to someone else? From a very early age, I learned motivation is a personal responsibility. Let me explain.

I grew up in Houston, Pennsylvania, a small town twenty-five miles south of Pittsburgh in a large Italian family. With a caring mom, a twin sister, and more uncles, aunts, and cousins than I could count, I experienced a wonderful, loving childhood. When I was ten years old, my father passed away. While it left a huge hole in my heart, his absence taught me at an early age that I had to be self-sufficient and that my own personal motivation would determine my destiny.

Upon arriving at the University of Dayton as a freshman, for the first time in my life, I was exposed to people from many different backgrounds. This exposure gave me a better frame of reference to measure myself from an educational, social, and leadership perspective. Again, I recognized my personal motivation would be key if I were to take advantage of the opportunity to grow and mature over the next four years.

After graduation, I enrolled in graduate school hoping to

get an MBA, but after a year, the money ran out. I joined the Air National Guard (this was during the Vietnam War) and spent the next eight months on active duty. After getting out of the armed services, I worked for Gillette as a sales rep, Rike's Department Store as an assistant buyer, and E.F. MacDonald as a creative writer. Each one of those experiences helped me develop relationships with senior executives, large clients, and some highly talented people. It was a combination of all of those experiences that motivated me to shape my personal and professional goals.

During that time, I coached wrestling at Carroll High School in Dayton with a college classmate of mine, Frank Chew. This program was only in its second year, the numbers were few and their experience was even less. What we were able to do with the program over a four-year period was quite amazing and gave me a great shot of confidence in my ability to influence an outcome. We led a bunch of young men who lacked skill and knowledge about wrestling, but made up for it with an enormous desire to learn. In four years, we built a program that was not only competitive in our area but soon became one of the elite programs in Southwest Ohio. With each of these experiences as part of my background, I truly understand that motivated people can accomplish anything.

OBSTACLE 2 Motivational Mix-Up

Armed with the belief that motivation was a personal responsibility, I was exposed to a very different approach in 1971 as a Berry sales rep. It was standard procedure in those early years to have sales meetings every day, including Saturday. I never quite understood the genesis of the meetings, but came to realize it wasn't about motivating the sales force but rather about a lack of trust. That same approach reappeared when I arrived in Buffalo in 1979. Our inability to hire people with a high probability of success and the poor performance in the New York division created a management style that fostered a lack of accountability and responsibility.

We held sales meetings every morning. They went something like this: I would stand up in front of our sales force and offer great inspiration like, "Ladies and gentlemen, I want you to know just how disgusted I am with your results over the last several weeks. The good news is . . . it's a new day. In fact, I want you to think about this as the first day of the rest of your life. And I want you to go out and sell, sell, sell! And if you don't, it will be the last day of the rest of your life. Now go get 'em, team!" The situation had deteriorated to the point where we held these meetings every morning and every evening; it was the Perfect Storm.

The response was understandable and overwhelming: resentment from those who were motivated, indifference from those who weren't.

Then, something amazing happened. As we got better at recruiting and hiring, the salesroom began to fill up with people who had a high probability of being successful. During these daily sales meetings, there was no longer resentment or indifference but rather puzzlement. The body language simply said, "Just tell us what you want us to do, and we'll go do it!" Lesson learned.

Motivation is a personal responsibility. Far too often we assume it is our responsibility to motivate our employees, our athletes, our children, our friends. But that assumption is wrong. Motivating

others is not our responsibility— period. If individuals can't get out of bed each and every morning excited about what the day promises, it's no one else's responsibility.

Lou Holtz is a real favorite of our family as a result of the personal interest he took in our son Peter and one of his friends while they were students at Notre Dame. Over the years, I've had a chance to talk to Coach Holtz and have heard him say many times that while "people often accuse me of being a great motivator, all I ever did was recruit motivated young men and teach them how to play football."

We closed the previous chapter with the statement that if you don't love what you do, you probably won't be very good at it. Restated, **"Your level of motivation is in direct proportion to the pleasure you receive from whatever you do."** It's where personal motivation starts and ends.

I had eleven bosses in thirty-three years with The Berry Company and not once did any of them ever call me up to ask

Motivation Is a Personal Responsibility

•

Inspiration Is the Responsibility of Others

how I felt and if I was excited about coming to work that day. That was my responsibility. Now, admittedly, I didn't walk around singing "Heigh-ho, heigh-ho, it's off to work I go. I am so merry because I work for Berry." Sure, some days were better than others. Ultimately, we can only be highly motivated

for each day when we accept accountability for ourselves.
We must recognize that when the right talent is properly aligned with the right opportunity, personal motivation is a natural outcome.

During our business transformation in 1981, we asked ourselves, if it's not our responsibility to motivate our employees, then what is our role? **Our conclusion was we need to care about them.**

Earlier, I referenced the work we've done at the University of Dayton's Center for Leadership & Executive Development in terms of applying Goleman's *Emotional Intelligence* (EI). If you share my belief that the caring side of the model truly defines those very special people in our lives, what is the one thing they all had in common? The answer is they provided us our greatest inspiration.

To properly ground this discussion, allow me to offer my definition of inspiration: Those people who have convinced us we could be more than we could be and have taken us to places we never thought we could go. It's those people who have believed in us more than we believe in ourselves.

When I ask my audiences to name the people who have been the greatest inspiration in their lives, the responses include parents, siblings, teachers, coaches, priests, ministers, rabbis, and friends. When I ask them what was the one thing they all had in common, the answer is: "They cared about me, they loved me." Employees are no different from our children.

They just want to know we care! It's the love word again. If we can transfer it from the home to the workplace, many employee issues can be solved. **Inspiration evolves from caring. It's not the vulnerable side people see, but rather the human side.** The fear that performance will be compromised becomes a non-issue when we recognize that love always has consequences associated with it. Call it tough love, but people have to know we care!

During the last two years, I've had the privilege of speaking at Marty Grunder's amazing boot camp for landscapers from all over the world. Marty, a very successful landscaper, businessman, and good friend has become a high priest of the landscaping industry and has been instrumental in many success stories as a result of his efforts and his caring approach.

During a Q&A, one of the participants asked me if as long as he paid his employees a fair wage, why was he obligated to do any more than that. He was really uncomfortable with the word love. My response was while it's certainly not a requirement to care about your folks beyond a paycheck, it then becomes unreasonable to ask them to care about you when times get tough.

Discoveries

1 Your level of motivation is in direct proportion to the pleasure you receive from whatever you do. We must recognize that when the right talent is properly aligned with the right opportunity, personal motivation is a natural outcome.

2 Inspiration is simply about caring about your employees, your athletes, your children, and your friends and convincing them they can be more than they can be. Inspiration will take them to places they never thought they could go.

CHAPTER FOUR

Leaders Provide Support

The next step in the journey begs the question: If we bring people into the business who have a high probability of being successful and we make certain to engage them in a caring relationship, what's next? Not unlike raising our own children, we need to clothe them, feed them, and provide for them. Using that analogy, it became clear that **leaders have to make absolutely certain their employees have the tools they need to be successful.** While that seems to be the natural order in any relationship, it is far too often not the case.

In *First, Break All the Rules*, Buckingham and Coffman state that the second question employees asked after "What is expected of me?" was "Do I have the materials and equipment I need to do my work right?" We were asking that same question seventeen years earlier and it became the second tenet of "The Leadership Pledge." When we asked ourselves how we were doing, the answer was "not very well."

OBSTACLE 3
Role Relationship Mix-Up

Back in 1981, we were still a family-held company. While Mr. L.M. Berry had lived to be ninety years old, his son, John Berry Sr., had really taken the leadership role of the company back in the mid-'60s. I'm not sure John ever got the credit he deserved for his role in the company's growth, but there's no question everyone inside the business knew of his contributions.

While employee appreciation was part of our heritage, employee engagement was scarce. We were still very hierarchical and employee input was minimal. Here's how we viewed our company:

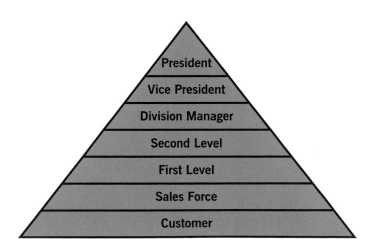

As we discussed how to give our employees the tools to do their jobs, it was obvious the old model was not practical. When we asked ourselves who were the most important people in our business lives, the overwhelming response was our customers and our advertisers. When we asked who were the people in the organization influencing our customer, the answer was the sales force.

In 1981, we introduced the Upside-Down Pyramid to the New York Division.

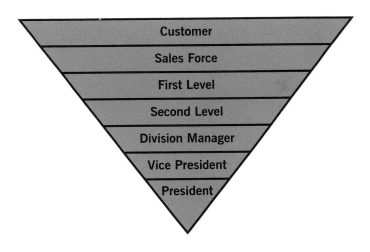

It answered the one fundamental question of our organization hierarchy: If you are not selling yellow pages, what is your role in the organization? Whether you are the switchboard operator or the president, everyone in the organization not directly selling to the advertisers was supporting the sales effort.

Salespeople interact with the customer every day, and so there was no one better to determine customer needs and expectations than the sales force.

Effective Leaders Manage Support Systems

•

Effective Employees Manage Themselves

What should be obvious to all of us is that leaders *lead* people and *manage* things. When we focus our energy on managing employee time and productivity, we become a victim of the employee's lack of focus. Every minute we spend managing someone's time and productivity takes away from our ability to support their needs. It's such an easy trap to fall into because as leaders, we are expected to influence the outcome.

As I've addressed this issue over the years from a corporate perspective, I would occasionally ask a handful of employees, "How do you get home at night and back to work in the morning without hurting yourself? Because you are totally helpless and useless from eight to five." They are the few I like to describe as "enthusiastically incompetent." They tell you, "Put me in, coach," and it goes straight down hill from there.

Now, the good news is most people do not come to work every day trying to bring the organization down. They want to do the right thing, and by the way, most of the answers reside with them. So, how effective are we at creating feedback loops? **As leaders and employees, we all have a responsibility for managing our half of the relationship.** The role of the CEO at The Berry Company was not much different from the role in other industries. Despite the many responsibilities of the position, none was more important than making certain my seven direct reports had what they needed to be effective in their most critical roles. All managers must embrace that same responsibility to be successful in meeting the needs of the customer. **One could make a strong argument that the most important level for that interchange to take place is at the supervisory level in all organizations. The majority of our employees report to that level and the supervisor's influence cannot be discounted either in performance or communication.**

I can't help but heap praise on The Berry Company in this

arena. In the late '70s, Charley Hughes and Vince Flowers from the Center for Values Research assisted Bill Tripp, our HR VP, in instituting a formal attitude survey process. We became much better at "listening and responding." With ninety-eight percent of our employees consistently saying they are proud to work for the company, we created wonderful feedback loops, both formal and informal, that fostered employee engagement.

Since retirement, I've heard concerns from senior managers and employees when it comes to this tenet. The first question I'm often asked is, "What if you can't respond favorably to what employees are asking for? How soon do you lose your credibility?" There is no question: If you are going to ask employees what they need to be effective at their job, then you have an obligation to respond. The answer is simple: **There is a significant difference between what employees want and what they need. It is the leader's decision to make those choices. Then, the leader must communicate these decisions. Remember, people can handle the truth and they will be reasonable as long as they understand. It's what isn't told to people that gets leaders into trouble.**

Elmer Smith, who preceded me as president, was the most effective leader I ever witnessed in this area. While his strategic sessions were quite often uncomfortable for those who weren't prepared, he was masterful at the prioritization of resource allocation. What everyone involved wants to know is that you are strategically positioning your resources for success.

The second question I'm often asked is about frequency. I've had a number of CEOs tell me with great pride that they have employee communication sessions at least twice a year. While I'm encouraged that they are listening, the bigger question is how much time do these same CEOs devote to informal communication both with their employees and their customers? **I've long believed that critical decisions are not made from corner offices. They are the result of all of us being more diligent about spending time in the field, in the plant, or wherever the bulk of our employees are located.**

I was fortunate to grow up in a company that put an incredibly high value on not only caring about employees but also recognizing they are the ones who ultimately define organizational greatness.

The third question often asked of me by employees at all levels of organizations is, "How can I make sure my voice is heard, and will it make a difference?" First and foremost, you've got to be in an organization that values your opinion. I caution the MBA students I teach and work with that when they are evaluating where they want to start their careers, they need to discern whether the company they want to work for values employee engagement. While most companies today are much more effective in employee engagement, their effectiveness is totally dependent on people's willingness to be involved.

Honest feedback is everyone's responsibility. In our MBA strategic capstone course we use an article by Jon Katzenbach from the *McKinsey Quarterly* titled "Real Change Leaders." Katzenbach suggests real change leaders (RCLs) are seldom found in executive suites. Though top-level involvement is essential, as previously discussed, the real change leaders who affect how the majority of people perform come from the ranks of middle and frontline managers. It's everyone's responsibility.

One last question was raised by a manager during a leadership conference for Growmark, a large farm co-op in Bloomington, Illinois. She asked, "How important is upward communication in your relationship with your boss?" My answer: **Communication, especially upward communication, is a critical component in any boss-employee, coach-athlete, and parent-child relationship.** I adopted a philosophy very early in my career with all of my bosses, which could be described this way: If I was in the water sinking, they were not going to be on the dock watching. We were going down together!

Being assertive in developing relationships with superiors is an absolute must. I've always found that putting my thoughts on paper (e-mail today) was a most effective way of communicating those critical issues. My former boss and dear friend Don Perozzi swore he kept each of my memos to him and re-read them if for no other reason than pure entertainment. (Got to make them interesting!)

There were also times when I failed to communicate effectively and it seriously hampered my and the company's success. One that I will always regret was my relationship with John Berry Jr., who I reported directly to from 1988 until 1994 as vice-president of the South Central line of business. My lack of communication with John Berry Jr. caused a huge rift between us in terms of his perception of my loyalty to the company. As the grandson of our founder and only the fifth president of The Berry Company, John's love for the company and the employees was unmatched. While in my heart I knew my loyalty never waned, split loyalties created this unhealthy relationship and it was a painful lesson. **It is always our personal responsibility to manage the relationship we have with our superiors.** Although over the years our relationship has been restored, I often wonder how much better it could have been.

I encourage our graduate students to recognize that the relationship with their professors is one that *they* must pursue if they are going to get the most out of the experience. My point is simple: If they don't know that you care, why should they care?

Discoveries

1 We have the responsibility as leaders to make absolutely certain our employees have what they need to be successful at what they do. As leaders, you must create effective feedback loops to engage employees in determining what they need to be effective.

2 It is a leader's responsibility to provide a support system and not over-manage relationships, thus becoming victims of their lack of focus. Consistent and constant communication and interaction by leadership must be a priority.

CHAPTER FIVE

Leaders
Set
Specific
Expectations

CUSTOMER SERVICE

VALUE FOCUSED

RELATIONSHIP SALES

What is it that we want from our employees, and what should they expect from us as bosses? How about asking the same question as parents, as friends, as spouses? The list goes on. I'm convinced all **relationships flourish or fail simply based on a clear (or unclear) understanding of what we expect from one another. Leaders need to clearly define and communicate expectations**

Recently, we were fortunate to have Dr. Charles E. Dwyer, professor at the Wharton School of Business and author of *The Shifting Sources of Power and Influence* visit the Center for Leadership & Executive Development as a guest lecturer. For more than forty years, Dr. Dwyer has written and lectured extensively on his belief that it is the behaviors and values of individuals within the organization that in turn drive the behaviors and values of the organization.

Dr. Dwyer says, "When all your values are clear in your mind, only then can you move to the more rewarding task of appealing to the values of others in order to influence their behaviors in a way that satisfies your values."

We only get what we want when we help other people get what they want. The more closely those two perspectives are aligned, the greater the chance we have of being successful.

As we thought about how to more clearly define expectations at Berry, we ran into our next obstacle.

 # Too Many Rules

It's important to spotlight the difference between rules and procedures. Procedures are necessary in every organization to insure your customers get what they want. These can vary depending on the business, but they need to be set, communicated, and followed. At The Berry Company, our procedures were all centered on making absolutely certain the ad got in the book correctly and accurately. I could spend a whole chapter sharing horror stories that happened in our business when these procedures were not followed. But except for the old adage about misery loving company, there's not much to learn here except it hurt. And so, to avoid pain, your procedures must be crystal clear as the absolute requirement to get the work done right.

Rules are different. When I'm addressing audiences, I ask, "Why do we have rules?" It is a set-up question because there is no correct answer. The responses usually range from maintaining order, assuring consistency, preventing chaos, and so on. While well intentioned, these responses are all wrong. Rules are created because somebody screwed up. What's worse, by the time the new rule is enacted, that individual is often long gone.

You know the question: "So, why do we do it that way?" The answer is, because we've always done it that way. I love the story about the little girl who walked into the kitchen and asked her mother why she was cutting off the ends of the ham before she put it in the pan. Her mother replied that she wasn't quite sure but her mother taught her to do it that way. Go ask her. The little girl ran to her grandmother and asked her why she taught her mother to cut off the ends of the ham before she put it in the pan. Her grandmother replied that she wasn't quite sure, but she remembers her mother taught her to do it, and she should go ask her. (Since I'm Italian, the great-grand-mother's name is always Nona, and they're always in the back bedroom in their rocking chair.) So, the little girl ran into Nona's bedroom and asked why she taught her grandmother who in turn taught her mother to cut off the ends of the ham before she put it into the pan. The great grandmother said very matter-of-factly, "Because the pan was too small!"

What a wonderful example of why we have rules! Given the top-down management style I described earlier, we had plenty. Let me give you another example. This one really did happen.

During a critically needed overhaul in Buffalo, the result of not meeting revenue expectations and the need to replace several managers, we transferred a new telephone sales manager, Rita Snyder, into our division. A couple of weeks later, Rita came to my office with a problem. One of our telephone sales reps, Phyllis Doherty, was arriving every day to work at 8:15 a.m., which was fifteen minutes past the required start time. Rita had several conversations with her, but nothing had changed.

What complicated the situation was that Phyllis was a tough-minded woman from south Buffalo, an eleven-time President's Club winner and our best rep. Her routine was the same every day. She arrived at 8:15 a.m., went to the salesroom, got a cup of coffee, and smoked two Lucky Strikes. She finally got started working at 9 a.m. and consistently sold lots of advertising.

After several discussions with Rita, I suggested either we accept the fact that Phyllis wasn't going to change, or we had to fire her. For all of the obvious reasons, neither of us believed firing her was an option. We came up with a third option. We asked permission to try a flexible work schedule. Employees could begin their day between 7 a.m. and 9 a.m. and finish between 3:30 p.m. and 5:30 p.m., the only requirement being they worked a forty-hour week. This approach not only solved our problem with Phyllis, it was eventually rolled out as a company-wide policy and had far reaching implications in our ability to meet the needs of a changing workforce.

In *First, Break All the Rules*, the authors suggest that creating a culture of compliance, that is, a company burdened by rules, slowly strangles the organization's flexibility, responsiveness, and perhaps most importantly, goodwill. My definition gets straight to the heart of the issue: **Rules are anything that get in the way by suffocating people's creativity, ingenuity, and spontaneity.**

In all likelihood, you already know the rules at work or home that get in the way—rules that exist to ensure minimal performance and inhibit individual creativity.

Standards of excellence are a completely different matter. **Standards of excellence encourage maximum performance and trumpet individual ingenuity.** They are gold-standard objectives that define great organizations from sports dynasties to General Electric and everything in between. Uncompromised standards of excellence create a greatness that is envied by competitors but seldom duplicated.

I love the story of the sculptor who created a beautiful angel out of marble. When people asked him how he sculpted such a magnificent work of art, he said simply, "I cut and chipped away everything that didn't look like an angel." Once these standards of excellence are defined, they must be communicated throughout the entire organization. **Remember, the solidarity of intent fills the team with the strength of knowing its purpose.**

Rules Are for the Weak

•

Uncompromised Standards of Excellence Are for the Strong

When I became president and CEO of The Berry Company, the business editor of the *Dayton Daily News* visited my office for an interview. He asked me the question that haunts every CEO: "What keeps you up at night?"

In an attempt at humor I used Lou Holtz's great response.

I said, "Nothing. I sleep like a baby. I wake up every two hours and cry." My real answer was, "Every morning, 2,800 Berry people wake up. It's halftime and we're down 13-6 and we're going to get after someone."

I added, "We do two things at The Berry Company. We sell yellow pages and we satisfy customers. Everyone in the organization knows that. Every strategy in our business aligns with those two fundamental purposes. Those two goals are why we turn the lights on in all of our offices, from Anchorage, Alaska, to Birmingham, Alabama, each and every morning. That's why we're still here successfully serving the telephone industry after nearly one hundred years. We've never lost our focus!"

Larry Taylor, the BellSouth officer who directed the consolidation of The Berry Company, and a man for whom I have enormous respect, reminded us in his letter of introduction that embracing simplicity is the clearest form of self-expression. Within an organization that is focused squarely on behavior, people must clearly understand their individual roles and responsibilities to insure success. Wise man! Larry also related this to me: "There's no limit to the good a man can do if he doesn't care who gets the credit."

An effective standard of excellence is simply one that creates a sustainable competitive advantage. How do we perform differently and better?

It wasn't until I retired and started teaching strategy in

University of Dayton's MBA Capstone program that I realized how effective The Berry Company's standards of excellence were. I've become convinced that some business schools and certain consultants are to blame for America's obsession with strategic planning. It's been my experience that eighty percent of our class time is devoted to strategy formulation and twenty percent to execution. I ask our students to promise me that after graduation when they get to the real world, they will devote twenty percent of their time to strategy formulation and eighty percent to execution of the strategy.

The number of organizations that are forever paralyzed in the strategy formulation phase is troubling. Becoming obsessed with quarterly reviews and their political ramifications or performing strategic gymnastics can take you away from what you need to be focused on: the customer.

As executive vice president, and later as president, I made it a priority to "graduate" all of our sales training classes. It was important that each of our new sales reps understood what they could expect from us as a company and what would be expected of them. Simply stated, I communicated that we expected them to sell lots of advertising and satisfy every customer. I also made it clear that if they weren't successful in doing both, at some point in their careers, they would no longer be employees of The Berry Company. I reminded them that while there are a number of strategies and tactics supporting that standard, the day we stop doing it better than everyone else would be the day we stop being the best.

How do we satisfy the customer? I remember vividly when Thomas J. Peters's *In Search of Excellence* came out in the late '80s. Suddenly, business people around the world were enlightened that the customer was important. I was shocked. Of course the customer is all important. From our point of view, that always had been and always will be true. We have a 1939 document from Mr. Berry that says our goal was simply creating "the largest amount of revenue consistent with the best subscriber relations." **The customer ultimately defines your success.**

I have an acquaintance who is CEO of a billion-dollar company that has struggled for a number of years. When you call their main number, you get a recording. If you do not know the extension of the person you are calling and you can't spell the name, it is impossible to talk to a human being. The company is losing millions of dollars every quarter and suffers from a shrinking customer base. I've asked him more than once, why can't you get someone to answer your phone? You never know, they may even want to buy something!

I have another close friend, John Blust, who owns Riffle and Associates, an electrical distribution business. Even though I know nothing about that field, through our friendship I have met a number of his employees and customers. He is universally loved by both . . . because he takes the time to care about both.

No matter what field you are in, ask yourself the following question: Does your organization have a clear understanding of its responsibilities and are there uncompromised standards of excellence that are clear to everyone? To quote Lord Chesterfield, "Whatever is worth doing at all, is worth doing well."

Discoveries

1 Creating a culture of compliance slowly strangles the organization of flexibility, responsiveness, and goodwill. Rules are anything that get in the way of creativity, ingenuity, and spontaneity.

2 Relationships flourish based on a clear understanding of expectations between one another. Enterprises fail when expectations are not clear.

CHAPTER SIX

Leaders Create Leaders, Not Followers

I believe greed is the single biggest problem we face as a society today. It is at the root of so many of the problems—from a broken political system, to a dysfunctional family structure, and everything in between. Greed has permeated organizations from youth sports teams to Fortune 100 companies. CEOs and politicians have been sentenced to prison, professional athletes are more juiced than Florida, and youth sports coaches and parents have twisted Vince Lombardi's pep talks into an impossible standard for the players.

The extremes are unfathomable. What drives a youth baseball coach to pay a nine-year-old to hit a teammate (who happened to suffer from mild autism) so he would be kept off his team? What possible rationalization could Bernie Ebbers, Richard Schrushy, or Kenneth Lay have created when they almost single-handedly destroyed WorldCom, HealthSouth, Enron, and thousands of people's lives in the process? How could top professional athletes like Barry Bonds, Mark McGwire, and so many others inject steroids into their bodies to gain a competitive edge, knowing that if they were discovered they would tarnish all of the their accomplishments as well as the game itself?

We already know the answer: Winning at all costs!

So, it begs the question: **How do we, either individually or collectively, avoid the trap of compromising our core values when pursuing our goals?** The answer, of course, is by focusing on behavior.

OBSTACLE 5 Management-Driven Standards

After we make certain our people know what is expected of them, we encounter the next obstacle: "management-driven standards." One of the many fallouts of any top-down-driven organization is the "I say, you do" approach to expectations. When that approach is applied, it influences everything the company does. Far too often, this mindset leads to organizational failure.

Athletic teams are judged by their wins and losses as obvious indicators of success or failure. Business organizations are benchmarked by profitability and are often victims of a lack of commitment to their own standards of excellence. One might argue that financial considerations define the end game.

The bigger issue is understanding how this lack of commitment to a standard of excellence does not compromise your core values. Where does it come from, who owns it, and is it doable?

The obsession with winning at all costs and personal greed puts so much strain on organizations for quarterly earnings that Wall Street has become the ultimate decision maker on what is acceptable performance. Frankly, Wall Street doesn't care about anything except profits. **You need to safeguard your people and your organization by making certain everyone is focused on behaviors that reflect the standards of excellence.**

There is plenty of effort put toward the strategic planning process, financial modeling, and objective setting. Far too often, an organization's goal is a top-down-driven number that is arrived at by financial analysts charged with growing the stock price and, eventually, management compensation.

That very notion almost caused my undoing. As mentioned earlier, The Berry Company is contracted by telephone companies to sell and publish their yellow pages. Unfortunately, because of the extremely high margins for the telephone company's yellow pages revenue stream, we frequently received unrealistic year-end goals. As the yellow page revenue stream became more significant in the '80s and '90s, the pressure grew.

To provide some perspective, the first yellow page directory was published in New Haven, Connecticut in 1879, and in the course of the next one hundred years, yellow pages revenue grew to one billion dollars. From 1980 to 1990, it grew from one billion dollars to eight billion dollars. Today, the industry generates roughly fifteen billion from the print and electronic directories.

When the situation in Buffalo took place, AT&T was still in control of the Baby Bells, and so the same business model was applied in all markets. New York Telephone made the decision to establish a goal of 19.81 percent growth in revenue. (It just happened to be the year 1981. Lots of thought went into setting that objective, huh?) It was the first time that, in a leadership position, I was confronted with an unrealistic set of expectations . . . and I handled it poorly. As I look back, we certainly didn't embarrass ourselves by growing the market 16 percent, but because it was less than the 19.81 percent budgeted increase, I was devastated. That's when the whole thing started to unravel for the New York Division and for me.

During my visit to Texas for that fateful week, Vince and Charley taught me about "ownership." They said if people own a little bit of the action and if they have some skin in the game, they treat the standards of excellence much differently. These standards now become their goal, their objective, their opportunity, and ultimately their victory. That simple piece of advice led me to the conclusion that great leaders create leaders, not followers.

The deeper you can drive leadership into an organization, the greater the chance you'll be successful. Leadership is more than a title or a designation.

We must displace the belief that leadership is the unwanted burden of the self-serving, dishonest, power-hungry elite we described

earlier, and replace it with an inspired acceptance that the gift of leadership is our most basic birthright.

The essence of leadership is about making responsible choices.

Leadership belongs to all of us.

Over time, I began to realize that it was virtually impossible to expect people to accept the responsibility of leadership unless their environment encouraged and acknowledged their efforts. I struggled with how to communicate this much-needed sense of ownership (leadership) among our employees. I questioned what role leaders should play in creating an environment where employees take responsibility for success and failure, not only for their respective work groups, but more importantly, for themselves and each other.

Leaders need to be more like a teacher than a boss. Leaders have to help employees confront difficult questions, issues, and challenges as they seek the right answers. By focusing on behavior, leaders create an environment in which candidness, courage, and caring about the company become every employee's responsibility. **As leaders, we must help our employees find within themselves the courage and clarity to lead others.** This is central to organizational success.

Ultimately, we realized creating that ideal environment had to start with us. It had to be demonstrated by our leadership team before we could expect the rest of the organization to do the same.

In 1997, we introduced "The Leader Transition Model" to The Berry Company, an initiative for senior management to give our employees a reason to want to come to work each and every day. First, **we had to provide them with a sense of purpose and an environment where they could grow personally and professionally.** It was our responsibility to communicate a vision bigger than one individual while still encouraging each person to understand the importance he or she played in the company's future.

Second, **leaders must display commitment**. The strength of the leader's commitment unleashes the power of the team. Don Blohowiak, founder of the Lead Well Institute, identifies the levels of commitment, starting with the saboteur as the least committed and the fanatic as the most committed. The Berry Company was full of fanatics at every level of leadership, so displaying commitment came naturally.

The next responsibility is externalizing passion. Put simply: "You can't lead where you're not willing to go." One of my favorite notes I received upon retirement came from a supervisor in our publishing office in Dayton, Angie Malloy. Angie wrote, "You taught us that passion grows exponentially when you invest it in the people you love in pursuit of a common goal."

If you aren't passionate about what you do, you just won't be very good at it. There is nothing more important than leaders displaying their love for what they do and the people they do it with. Not only is it infectious, it's an absolute requirement.

The next step is where the magic begins. **Great leaders create leaders, not followers.** I'm certain this can be debated with regularity but I'll have no part of it. I go back to something we were taught early in our careers as young Berry managers: the Pygmalion Effect. Pygmalion was a mythological king who lived on the island of Cyprus. As the story goes, Pygmalion built a sculpture of a woman with such beauty and grace that he fell in love with it. More than anything else, he wanted the statue to come to life, so he prayed to the Greek goddess of love, Aphrodite. His prayers were answered as his sculpture, Galatea, came to life as a woman of incredible warmth and beauty. He and Galatea married and lived happily ever after.

The Pygmalion effect describes the power of expectation. **If we communicate the vision, coupled with the expectations, people are drawn to those expectations.** That was the storyline for the movie *My Fair Lady* with Audrey Hepburn. "Treat me like a lady, I'll become a lady; treat me like a tramp and I will follow suit." As we communicate our expectations of others, we influence their expectations of themselves. When we expect our employees to act and behave as leaders, they fulfill these expectations.

Organizations Will Experience Meaningful Success When People Establish Their Own Standards of Performance

It has long been my belief that our very best people determine our organizational greatness. **Great leaders create heroes, and heroes become the standard of excellence.** Each year, we would negotiate (that's really a stretch) with our parent BellSouth to determine our net income requirement and we would ultimately be told what was required to feed that big bulldog in Atlanta. Of course, the next step in the process was for each of our four lines of business to be given their net income requirement (not much negotiation there either) and they in turn would distribute their objective among their respective divisions.

As mentioned earlier in this chapter, despite a great deal of time dedicated to strategic planning and financial modeling, the requirements of our parent and our telephone customers were always the highest priority. I can assure you that in most companies, that same exercise in futility is the norm, not the exception. At the end of the day, whatever is determined as the number has little to do with whether or not it will be achieved. That's where the essence of leadership—making responsible choices—comes into play. In any organization the best people continually achieve a level of performance that in most instances exceeds the expectations of its leaders. Each year, we recognized our top sales people through the annual Excellence 110 awards. Never less than a third of our attendees were multiple winners and many had been for ten years or more. Those sales leaders truly establish the standard of excellence in any organization. **They are the heroes who ultimately define organizational greatness.**

Why do organizations struggle? Each one has heroes who bring their best every day, as well as a group of average performers. So, then, is it the non-performers that drive mediocrity, that rob American corporations, education, non-profits and sports programs of their chance for success? The answer is yes, and no. While it's the non-performers' behaviors that neutralize the organization, more damaging is the reluctance of the organization's leaders to confront poor performance.

The unwillingness to confront poor performance at all levels of organizations shocks me, even more than leaders' lack of focus on the hiring process, as I've visited so many different operations since I've retired. It's back to the paradox of unconditional love versus conditional love (tough love).

Who are we really trying to protect? In his book, "Winning Ways," Jack Welch address the issue head-on when he says, "Classic philosophers like Kant give powerful arguments that not being candid is actually about self-interest, making your life easier." I would take it one step further—I believe it's the ultimate act of selfishness.

What does it look like when we are not willing to confront non-performers, and more importantly, what does it look like when we do? Here's an illustration:

Performance of 20 Salespeople

	Situation A	Situation B	Situation C
Above Average	5	5	7
Average	10	15	13
Below Average	5	0	0

Let's first look at Situation A. It's almost universal that five of the twenty are our heroes, those who always deliver above-average performance. The ten in the middle could be described as average. The bottom five are just that—below average non-performers. There are only two reasons why these five are at the bottom of the grid: they either can't or they won't. It's either aptitude or attitude. In most instances, the bottom five aren't bad people, but their talent just doesn't align with the requirements of their job. What's worse is the amount of time managers spend with these non-performers trying to make them something they're not. Remember, skill and knowledge can be developed. Talent cannot. Therefore, most managers continue to ask people to keep working at their skill level, and when they fail to achieve the impossible goal of converting non-talent into talent they become the problem. Bad attitudes result as the persistence focused primarily on non-talent is wasted.

Because organizations refuse to confront the five poor performers, they neutralize the five heroes, and the organization as a whole becomes very average. It's simple: Those five non-performers have got to go. Either up or out!

But when we do confront the non-performers, we can change the make-up to five heroes and fifteen average performers (Situation B). Now we have a chance

There was a time in my career when I thought everyone

was going to succeed at the highest level. They were all going to be heroes. What I learned (quite painfully, I might add) is great organizations are a blend of a bunch of average performers that show up every day and give it their best, plus a few who perform at the highest level. One only has to look at a successful baseball team to appreciate that blend. How many true stars fill a team's roster? (other than the Yankees, of course.)

So the question remains: how do you get to Situation C? How do we, as leaders, move those who have the capacity to operate at the highest level but for some reason are stuck in the average alley? The challenge lies in getting them to recognize that they have the capability to perform better, to be more than they currently are.

Jim Loehr, author of *The Power of Full Engagment* and one of our thought leaders at the Center, gets as close to answering this difficult question as anyone I've read. At their Human Performance Institute, located in Orlando, Florida, they train a wide spectrum of individuals, from professional athletes to Navy Seals to corporate executives. They understand that an individual "build the skills and capacity to remain fully engaged regardless of the conditions" in order to perform at the highest level possible. We must skillfully manage our personal resources, drawing from physical, emotional, mental and spiritual energy in order to do our best work.

As Jim says, these sources of energy are dependent on one another, there is nothing more important than ultimately recognizing that to "find meaning and purpose in what you do is the only real pathway to sustained levels of extraordinary productivity and achievement."

So to best frame Situation 3, we have to understand that the five who are operating at the highest level, leaders must provide great clarity to help them recognize their ultimate destination. And for the next two that could move up into the highest echelon, it's the leader's responsibility to help them understand that, in the words of Steve Prefontaine, the great long distance runner of the 60s, "to not give the best of ourselves each and every day is to sacrifice the gift." It is our responsibility as leaders, coaches, parents, professors, friends, and peers to show others that without clarity of purpose, they will always fall short!

First, you've got to convince them that better performance is in their best interest. You've got to spend time with them and understand their strengths and what makes them unique. While it's ultimately their choice, they need to understand the difference between wanting to win and hating to lose, the difference between being afraid to fail and fearing failure.

Too often overlooked is peer-to-peer influence. I have had the opportunity to work with a number of college athletes, and in particular, captains of varsity athletic teams. I'm constantly reminding them that the "C" on their chest does not stand for "captain" but rather for "courage." I also remind them that they have significant influence on one another, more than anyone else in fact, including their coaches, if and when they fully commit to a leadership role.

I'm reminded of a story that was told to me by a college soccer player who is now in the World Soccer League. In his senior year, his team failed to make it to the NCAA tournament, which was his dream. He was quite adamant that he didn't take his responsibility as captain seriously enough. Because of the team's unwillingness to make the commitment necessary to achieve the same goal, despite the fact that they possessed the talent, he allowed them to "steal the dream."

When we can create an environment that encourages employees to find within themselves the courage to lead, then and only then will they understand that by shaping the destiny of the organization, they will in turn establish their own standards of performance. It belongs to them. Top performance belongs to everyone.

Discoveries

1 If employees have ownership in the decision-making process, they will treat it like their own. We must understand that leadership is our most basic birthright. When we allow employees to be part of setting standards of performance, it's an admission that we acknowledge that the essence of leadership is about making responsible choices.

2 Great leaders not only create leaders but recognize that those heroes define the standard.

3 Leaders must confront poor performance. Not being candid is purely about self-interest and making our own lives easier.

CHAPTER SEVEN

Leaders Provide Honest Feedback

Let's quickly review what we've covered so far. First, you must hire people who possess both character and talent as well as have a high probability of being successful. To do this, you must make an honest appraisal of your own character and talent and realize these issues are how others will mark your scorecard.

Second, you must provide your employees with the tools to do the job.

Third, you must make absolutely certain everyone is clear on and understands what is expected from them.

And next? You must be committed to sharing feedback. Thus, the fourth tenet of the Management Creed: "Share Honest Feedback."

Back in 1981, I was focused on sharing with our people the qualities that define success. I sensed that to lead effectively I had to **help people understand the qualities that differentiate greatness.**

First, let's take a look at providing feedback (training and development) from a traditional point of view so you can see why it's so important to focus on this in a disciplined manner.

First, you must accept these beliefs:

- When we stop getting better, we stop being good.

- When we stop growing, we start dying.

- We know what we are, but not what we may be.

It is an absolute requirement that if you are going to tap into your God-given talent, you must diligently work at getting better every day.

This cannot be done alone. It requires constant feedback from bosses, parents, spouses, coaches, and friends. Let's spotlight this part of the discussion on professional development. As noted earlier, being in the right circumstance is a requisite to growth, but know that the same applies to your personal life as well.

Time and again, I was painfully reminded that it was not within the power of a boss, or a spouse, or any leader to train or develop talent. Everyone in business must recognize that an organization's success is determined by our effectiveness at hiring people into positions and responsibilities that align with their talents.

Therefore, you must commit to an effective selection process. Remember, you can teach skill and knowledge, but you can't teach talent.

At The Berry Company, we had a "quartile ratings" report, which was available to senior management. It was used to remind our field managers and trainers of the enormous cost of not only poor selection but proper utilization of training resources. The report tracked all our sales reps, measuring their performance in relation to their peers in their respective divisions at ten-year increments.

After the first year there was very little movement of the reps from quartile to quartile, regardless of length of service. This pattern suggested a high percentage of the learning curve, in terms of product knowledge and selling skills, happened within the first twelve months.

You need to know five simple and straightforward "truths" that apply to all organizations regarding training and development.

1. First, depending on the learning curve, employees settle into a specific comfort level after a certain amount of time. At that point, regardless of the amount of time spent in skill development, there appears to be a limit to influencing performance thereafter.

2. There is a window of time, depending on the industry, during which you can impact individual results. Our experience showed the first year of employment is the most critical time for professional development.

3. Third, most managers, when trying to transform employees beyond their capacity, ultimately spend an inordinate amount of time with those bottom-quartile performers who, as we discussed in the previous chapter, must go up or out!

4. Fourth, from an individual perspective, each of us must learn to separate our talent from our skill. If you have not found your sweet spot within the first year, there is strong evidence you simply are not in the right circumstance to max out your God-given talent.

5. Last, and most important, there must be a shift to balance selection with training in terms of time and resources. In most organizations, success is largely dependent on the effectiveness of the first-line supervisor and his or her ability to lead/manage the employees who interact with customers every day. Far too often, the first-line manager's job description is loaded with training responsibilities that result in shadowing poor performers for the purpose of terminating them from the business. Increased involvement to maximize the "heroes" and encourage the "middle of the road" performers to pursue "heroes" status, as well as more engagement in recruiting talent, would have a much greater benefit for the organization.

More effective hiring procedures reduce the ratio of time spent between manager and employee.

Now, back to the journey! At Berry, my interest in providing feedback was critical to helping our people understand the qualities that characterize top performers, the "heroes," in order to emphasize what defines organizational greatness.

OBSTACLE 6 — What Qualities Distinguish Greatness

What qualities do all winners have in common? Is it hard work? YES! Although, there was a time in my life when I thought that hard work was an attitude, I've come to understand that hard work is a skill. The willingness to work hard is the ticket allowing us play in the game. **Hard work is a prerequisite to personal success . . . but not a differentiator.**

Was it luck? The answer to that is also YES! Vince Lombardi's famous quote, "Luck is when opportunity meets preparation," says it so well. I believe luck is when the window opens for you to apply hard work.

While I do believe both hard work and luck are part of it, they are not the only factors. As I continued on my discovery journey, I kept searching for the answer. Was it attitude, concentration, desire, faith, integrity, motivation, persistence, responsibility, vision, wisdom? The answer was always YES! But, I knew it had to be more than that.

In 1984, I finally found the answer in this line from William Ian Graves:

"Winners do things that they don't like to do; average people only follow their natural likes and preferences."

I read this line again, and again, and again. Then I said, WOW!

Think about it. Have you ever accomplished anything of significance in your life without being out of your comfort zone? The answer is absolutely not! We've all participated in this semi-scary experience but how many of us have established it as a habit? Not many!

Intuitively, I believe most people in this world are average. In the Pete Luongo statistical world, I would suggest that seventy percent of the people in the world are average, ten percent are winners, and twenty percent fall into the bottom third, with fifteen percent of them suffering the indignity of being born into a circumstance that they can't get out of, and five percent, who could but won't (the worst kind).

Most people are average, and that's because they only do what they like to do. What separates the heroes from the rank and file? First, they are in the right circumstance, and second, they have established the habit of discipline. Said another way, **winners have established the habit of doing things they don't necessarily like to do, but because they recognize that it's an absolute requirement to accomplish those goals, they do them.** History is filled with thousands of examples. All of the winners I've known established the habit of doing things they didn't like to do as they pursued their goal.

All of us have learned from past experiences that there's a very real difference between great and insignificant. We all have been there when our overwhelming desire for success took us over the top, and likewise, when we perhaps backed down from that last step needed to achieve something and then felt the sting of falling short when we knew success was within reach.

I believe the reason "doing things we don't like to do" doesn't become part of who we are is because it isn't ingrained in our everyday lives. Until we have established that habit of discipline, we will continue to suffer the fate of wanting but not having.

What separates world-class athletes like Michael Jordan, Lance Armstrong, and Tiger Woods from their peers and helps them earn superstar status? Having the opportunity of getting to know Annika Sorenstam on a personal level confirmed my belief that the first distinguishing difference is discipline.

Here's a wonderful example of a unique individual who has established the habit of discipline and how it has impacted her life. It is part of who she is and how she lives every day.

Annika played in an LPGA event, the Starbank Classic at the Country Club of the North outside of Dayton, Ohio, for two consecutive years. As a resident of the club and a member of the tournament committee, Debbie and I had the privilege of hosting Annika as our house guest both of those years. Observing Annika prepare herself each day was truly a study in discipline. Her conditioning, preparation, concentration, and practice habits were all manifestations of discipline—her commitment to the physical and mental preparation that was uncomfortable, inconvenient, difficult, and challenging but an absolute requirement.

What I found most interesting was her transformation from a shy, unassuming, and extremely pleasant young lady off the course to a focused, determined, no-nonsense, fearless competitor whose sole objective was to win golf tournaments. From her stretching and workout regiment, diet, mental visualization, pre-round practice routine, and on-course preparation with her caddy Terry McNamara, to her post-round review sessions, all were incredible displays of doing things that I'm sure at times she would rather not be doing. These requirements are what drives Annika to become the greatest woman golfer to ever play the game.

Greatness Is Achieved by Those Who Have Established the Habits of Discipline and Risk Taking

Then just when I thought the journey of discovery had ended with the knowledge of the most important characteristic that separated the best from the rest, a strange thing happened. In the summer of 1989, I was watching the film *Dead Poets Society* and it hit me:

Carpe Diem . . . Seize the Day!

Voilà—the second part of the answer. **not being afraid to fail!** I became so enamored with the underlying message of the movie that I watched it several times.

This second key to distinguishing greatness became the theme for our business the following year. At our annual leadership conference, we sent movie tickets in advance to each attendee. When the group arrived for the opening night, we had converted the conference room at the Hyatt into a movie theater with all of the amenities of an opening night premiere.

Over the next two days, all of our managers participated in team-building exercises without one single mention of the movie or its purpose. On the closing day of the conference, we introduced our theme by showing sixteen vignettes from *Dead Poets Society* that addressed what I believe is the second inhibitor that holds people back . . . being afraid to fail. As William Shakespeare wrote so eloquently, "Our doubts are traitors and make us lose the good we oft might win by fearing to attempt."

I want to share three of those vignettes that articulate this powerful message. If you've seen the movie these scenes will resonate quickly. If you haven't seen it (and please do) let me provide some background:

Mr. Keating, played by Robin Williams, was an English teacher who had returned to his alma mater, Welton, a prep school in New England, to teach.

The first vignette that addressed the issue of "being afraid to fail" and introduced the theme "carpe diem," took place in one of the opening scenes when Mr. Keating welcomed the students to his class on the first day of school. He immediately ushered them into the lobby of the school where they stood in front of a trophy case. He asked Mr. Pitts, one of his students to recite from the poem "To the Virgins, to Make Much of Time," by Robert Herrick. "Gather ye rosebuds while ye may,/ Old time is still a-flying:/And this same flower that smiles to-day/Tomorrow will be dying." He told the students the Latin term for that sentiment was "carpe diem."

With that as background, he gathered all of the students in front of a trophy case that contained pictures of generations of former Welton students. With their eyes glued on the trophy case, he told them, "you've walked past them many times but you never really looked at them. Peruse some of the faces of the past. They had haircuts like you. They were full of hormones just like you. They were invincible just like some of you feel now. Gentlemen, did they wait until it was too late to make one iota of what their lives were capable of? You see, gentlemen, these boys are all now fertilizing daffodils. If you listen real close you can hear them whispering their legacy to you." And he whispered, "Carpe diem, seize the day. Boys, make your lives extraordinary."

The next vignette took place later in the movie when Mr. Keating jumped on his desk in the classroom and told his students, "I stand upon my desk to remind myself that we must constantly look at things in a different way." As they took turns jumping on the desk, he reminded them to "strive to find your own voice, gentlemen, and remember the longer you wait, the less chance you have of finding it." Then he quoted Thoreau, "Most men lead lives of quiet desperation," and told them, "Gentlemen, don't resign yourselves to that."

The third vignette involved Mr. Keating as he gathered all of his students in the courtyard and told them to walk any way they want. They quickly fall into a cadence as the others clapped. When they stopped, he told them that the purpose of this exercise was to illustrate conformity. Then he said, "All of us have difficulty maintaining our own beliefs in the face of others. We all have a great need for acceptance but we must trust that our beliefs are our own." Then Keating quotes Robert Frost: **"Two roads diverged in a wood and I—I took the one less traveled by, and that has made all the difference."**

Three vignettes, one constant theme, all speaking to my belief that the other half of what defines greatness is establishing the habit of risk taking. I believe the greatest tragedy in someone's life would be if the last five words out of their mouth were, "I wish I would have!"

Arnold Bennett, British novelist in the early 1900s maybe said it best: "The real tragedy is the tragedy of the man who never once in his life braces himself for that one supreme effort, who never stretches to his full capacity, never stands up to his full stature."

I empathize with people who feel trapped in this malaise. It almost became my undoing back in 1981. My obsession with winning almost destroyed me. As I've reflected on those very trying times over the years, I wondered if the problem was my obsession with winning or was it being afraid to fail? I'm not sure they can be separated. What I learned from that experience is that whatever good or bad fortune may come out of a circumstance, we can always give it meaning and transform it into something of value. There is a big difference between what's lost by not trying and what's lost by not succeeding. I've witnessed that truth many times in my life. I've seen it as a coach, an official, a sales manager, a leader, a friend, a professor, a board chair, and on and on and on. I've been on countless sales calls with outstanding salespeople who at the moment of truth could not ask for the order. As a coach and an official, I've observed hundreds of wrestling matches at all levels where world-class wrestlers arrive at that moment of truth and freeze on the mat. I've sat in hundreds of meetings and observed leaders at all levels avoid tough decisions because they were afraid of the outcome.

Teddy Roosevelt had it right in his book on leadership when he said, "Credit goes to the man in the arena whose face is marred by dust and sweat and blood: who strives valiantly . . . who knows the great enthusiasms, the great devotions, who spends himself in a worthy cause, who at the best knows in the end the triumph of high achievement, and who at the worst, if he fails, he fails while daring greatly, so that his place shall never be with those cold and timid souls who have never known victory nor defeat."

Failure is our teacher. Regret is our enemy. Failure is a natural consequence of trying. The point isn't whether we have failed or succeeded but rather what have we learned from it. It's been my experience that great leaders, great salespeople, and great athletes all have an incredibly high tolerance for failure because they recognize it provides them with their greatest feedback loop. Think about the experiences through which you learned the most. Probably your best lessons were learned not when you were successful, but when you failed to meet a goal or objective.

To gain a positive lesson from a failure, you must own the loss. You've got to fail in a learning posture. It only becomes valuable when it's treated as a measure of strength.

Let me share a personal experience that defines the experience. I was a wrestling coach at Carroll High School in Dayton, Ohio in 1969. We had just finished a very difficult season, but I knew we were getting close to discovering our greatness. Most of our athletes had only been wrestling for two or three years, but had made steady progress. Unfortunately, the first match of that year had been against our rival, power-house Beavercreek, and turned out to be our worst loss of the year. They shut us out 38-0. I decided to use that match as motivation for what I believed could be our best season in school history. I was not going to let these athletes forget that loss. In fact, I had a friend of mine crochet a throw rug in the Beavercreek colors of orange and black with the score—Beavercreek 38, Carroll 0—covering the entire rug. At every practice, each wrestler had to wipe his feet on that rug before he walked on the mat, a routine that served as a subtle reminder of what happened the previous season.

As we prepared to wrestle Beavercreek in our first match the following year, we were underdogs. I'm not sure anyone thought we could win the match . . . other than our thirteen wrestlers and our coaches. As we prepared to go upstairs to a sold-out gym, I brought the rug into the locker room. As they sat nervously waiting for last-minute instructions and encouragement, I simply threw the rug at them and asked them what they were going to do when they got upstairs. Well, the scene was bedlam as they ripped that rug into hundreds of pieces. Each of them tucked a tiny shred in his uniform and off we went.

Our athletes wrestled their best. So well, in fact, that we were behind only two points going into the last match which had we won (we didn't), would have clinched the victory. I can remember as if it were yesterday when Paul Martin, an outstanding football and wrestling coach, came up to me and said, "Your kids deserved to win tonight. They wrestled a hell of a match." My response was, "We did win, Paul, because tonight an entire group of young men learned that you can accomplish anything if you believe in yourselves and each other."

This story did not capture the headlines, and I doubt if many people remember what happened that night, but I can assure you that it serves as a great reminder that, on December 5, 1969, thirteen young men and a coach learned one of life's great lessons: there is no failure when a man has not lost his courage, his character, his self-respect, or his self-confidence.

Discoveries

1 Winners do things they don't like to do. Average people follow their natural likes and preferences.

2 Winners establish the habits of discipline and risk taking. They have no fear of failure. They recognize that failure provides the greatest feedback as long as they own the loss and fail in a learning posture.

3 Failure is our teacher. Regret is our enemy.

4 There is no comparison between what's lost by not trying and what's lost by not succeeding.

CHAPTER EIGHT

Leaders
Breed
Trust

As the journey at Berry continued, we asked the question, what's next? We'd already learned the importance of:

1. finding people who possess both character and talent and who have a high probability of being successful

2. providing them with the resources they need to be effective

3. telling them what was expected, and finally,

4. sharing meaningful feedback.

What was left? Our conclusion was simple and straight-forward: we had run out of things to do! It was a defining moment in the process.

One of the biggest obstacles in any successful relationship, professional or personal, is defining roles and responsibilities. As leaders, the tendency is to over-manage the relationship to get what we want, not recognizing that **you only get what you want when you help other people get what they want.**

This concept is more critical today than it was twenty-five years ago as gender equity, work-life balance, and a multitude of social issues have become a much greater part of our professional lives. **When there is no clear definition of roles and responsibilities, it's difficult to successfully manage to outcomes and solutions in any relationship.**

The lines have become blurred as to the rights and privileges we all believe we deserve. When we are uncertain about the obligations and responsibilities we have to our companies, bosses, peers, employees, and customers, we become doubtful and unfocused.

We must be accountable and responsible for our own performance. Anyone worth their salt not only wants this kind of relationship, but grows and prospers when they know what they're accountable for. But it's a paradox. **Regardless of whether the other person in a relationship is an employee, a peer, a customer, a supplier, a life-partner, or your teenage child, you can't ask them to be accountable and responsible for their behavior until you've accepted accountability and responsibility for managing your half of the relationship.**

Ultimately, we're all responsible for "Clarifying Boundaries and Increasing Freedom," which is one of the paradoxes in James R. Lucas's book, *Broaden the Vision and Narrow the Focus: Managing in the World of the Paradox*. Jim has been one of our most popular thought leaders at the Center for Leadership & Executive Development. His solution to this challenge, based upon years of research, supported and bolstered what we instinctively created as a better way for The Berry Company.

In his book, Jim writes, "At its best, leadership is aware of more than the bare-bones potential conflict between freedom and boundaries. We act on two mutually reinforcing ideas: there is no sustainable freedom without the guidance of reasonable boundaries, and there are no sustainable boundaries without the guidance of reasonable freedom."

He goes on to say, "If we hold both in our hands and exploit the tension between them we can have freedom that feels safe—and boundaries that feel free."

In a much more simplified approach, "reasonable boundaries" describes our responsibility as boss, parent, coach, or friend to put people in the best possible situation to maximize their talent, give them the resources they need to be successful, make our expectations clear, and provide positive, meaningful feedback. "Reasonable freedom" describes making sure they accept responsibility and accountability for their actions.

Back in Buffalo, while we had developed our five tenets, I struggled with how to help our people know what it looked like and felt like when they truly accepted accountability and responsibility. It still wasn't clear to me how to measure our success or failure in this area. Then, I heard Coach Lou Holtz, the former Notre Dame football coach, share his thoughts on this subject during one of his motivational speeches. I knew right then that two of those measurements resided in his advice.

In his book *Winning Every Day*, Coach Holtz says, "Before

ever choosing an action, ask yourself, will this elevate my opinion of myself? It all starts when you ask yourself three questions: Can I trust you, are you committed to excellence, and do you care about me?"

Following Coach Holtz's lead, I felt I was getting closer to knowing how to effectively measure accountability. Trust and commitment were a very natural fit, but we had made the third issue of caring about "me" (love) a prerequisite in the process long before we ever became concerned about measuring accountability. Intuitively, I knew the third one had to focus on our corporate culture. It was the most important part of what made The Berry Company a place where employees felt valued, respected, and part of something special. If we were going to preserve this special culture, then loyalty had to be the third leg on the stool that would define accountability.

And so the journey continued with the next obstacle:

OBSTACLE 7 **Lack of Trust**

Trust. Is there anything else more important in any relationship, professional or personal? The answer is an unequivocal no! In my early years at The Berry Company, a lack of trust was at the heart of how the business was managed. It was not in a mean-spirited way, but rather a result of a paternalistic management style that fostered dependency on the "boss" for some measure of self-esteem. It was a caste system that by its very nature encouraged a lack of trust and a management style prevalent in most corporate settings in the '50s, '60s, and '70s. Unfortunately, it's still prevalent in today's business climate, and the culprit is the unquenchable thirst for profit with little regard for the long-term health of the organization.

I want to re-visit each of the obstacles and truths presented to ground how trust, or lack of trust, permeated every decision, choice, and change we introduced as we traveled our journey.

As we experienced high turnover, our inability to hire people of strong character and talent immediately put us in the difficult position of confronting poor performance. **By its very nature, the inability to hire effectively breeds a lack of trust in every organization.** It comes down to one simple problem: the inability to produce results! When organizations become ineffective, the fallout will always end up in mistrust between managers, employees, and everyone else in between—including customers.

On the heels of poor hiring decisions came the belief that it was our responsibility to motivate employees, which descends directly from a lack of trust. **If an employee is not motivated, then they probably aren't in the right circumstance.** Any attempt of putting undue pressure to incite interest will almost always be met with resistance, ultimately ending in a trust trap.

Truth #3: "Effective Leaders Manage Support Systems. Effective Employees Manage Themselves." This truth gets to the heart of trusting your employees. As leaders and employees, the more effective feedback loops we create, the more engaged we are, and the more dependent we become on each other for solutions. Anything short of this undermines the entire organization, breeding a lack of trust at all levels.

The next obstacle, "Too Many Rules," is the most blatant violation of trust. Consider the first part of Truth #4, "Rules are for the weak." I caution each of you as bosses, or people responsible for others, to avoid the trap of creating a culture or relationship of compliance that slowly strangles the organization of individual flexibility, creativity, energy, and most importantly, trust.

The fifth obstacle "Management-Driven Standards" speaks to the notion that leadership is more than a title or designation, but rather our most basic birthright. Let me remind you that the essence of personal leadership is making responsible choices. The more we encourage our employees to own "a little bit of the action," the more we create an environment in which trust will flourish, and employees truly will define excellence. **Remember, ownership breeds engagement, its absence breeds contempt, and contempt is a synonym for a lack of trust.**

We've also examined how the feedback process must be administered effectively and accepted as meaningful. Marshall Goldsmith, named one of the top five executive coaches by both *Fortune* and the *Wall Street Journal*, spoke at the Center for Leadership & Executive Development during a day-long seminar titled, "What Got You Here Won't Get You There." In his book with the same name, he says, "Negative feedback often becomes an exercise in 'let me prove you wrong,' and far too often focuses on problems, shortcomings, and mistakes." Assuming we can influence behavior and the person is in the right circumstance, nothing can be more devastating than the kind of feedback Marshall described above. It will breach a trust in the relationship that in most instances will never recover.

If We Have No Trust, We Have No Relationship

I have a very simple belief when it comes to trust: If we have no trust, we have no relationship. There can be nothing more critical to successful relationships, individually or collectively, than the willingness to trust one another. We must recognize that we can't ask for what we're not willing to give. **Trust happens when leaders are transparent, candid, and keep their word.** While I had always perceived candidness as an asset, it wasn't until I learned to deliver it in a positive, caring manner that it became one of my greatest strengths. You must exemplify competence, character, and connection as a leader. Only when we learn to reach out to our bosses, our peers, and our employees for feedback can we truly develop trusting relationships. Sure, you have to make sound decisions, but when you're wrong you've got to be willing to admit it. Most importantly, you must put what's best for the people in your organization ahead of your personal agenda. As we discussed, in a world where greed and instant gratification have become prevalent, trusting relationships have dwindled. It's only when we earn trust from our bosses, our employees, our spouses, our children, our partners, and our friends that we can expect it in return.

When I went through the Buffalo experience, mistrust became part of my nature. I operated with the notion that "you have to earn my trust" and I became terribly cynical and distrustful. While there may be some roles in which cynicism and distrust are vital, it is a death wish for leaders.

Let's leave this section with a conclusion: **Before we ask ourselves if we are accountable for our actions and before we ask if others accept that same responsibility, we must ask, Can I be trusted?**

The survival rate without it is zero.

Discoveries

1 The inability to effectively hire breeds a lack of trust. If an employee is not motivated, any attempt of putting undue pressure to incite interest will always be met with resistance, ending in a trust trap. While encouragement breeds engagement, its absence breeds contempt and contempt is a synonym for a lack of trust.

2 When a lack of understanding of roles and responsibilities exists, it creates an obstacle to successfully managing outcomes and solutions in any relationship. We can't ask others to be accountable and responsible until we've accepted accountability and responsibility for managing our half of the relationship.

3 We can't expect trust until we earn it.

CHAPTER NINE

Leaders
Foster
Commitment

Commitment rarely comes without reciprocity. It comes from feeling necessary. By giving employees a sense of purpose and encouraging them to embrace a leadership role, we provide them with the opportunity to help shape the organization. **The strength of a leader's commitment unleashes the power of the team.**

Here we focus on commitment as part of accepting personal accountability and responsibility and defining it as the second characteristic in measuring both. It's more than reasonable to expect people to embrace commitment, but it is a personal choice. What got me into trouble in 1981 was my complete lack of understanding that commitment is a personal choice.

In my attempt to inspire our employees to develop the traits I believed they lacked, I put commitment at the top of the list. I was obsessed with helping our people understand what real commitment looked like, and I made myself the example they needed to emulate.

When we brought in Don Blohowiak, president of The Lead Well Institute, to help us better understand "our culture," (the phrase employees often used when asked what made The Berry Company special), Don also introduced us to a commitment continuum, which assigned levels from the least committed (saboteurs) to most (crusaders and fanatics).

OBSTACLE 8 Lack of Commitment

The Commitment Continuum

Least Committed ⟶ Most Committed

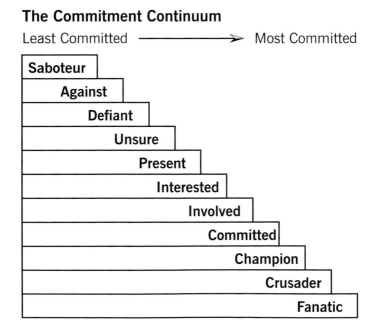

Saboteur

Against

Defiant

Unsure

Present

Interested

Involved

Committed

Champion

Crusader

Fanatic

My view, back in 1981, was that I was the most committed (fanatic) without question, with a few who charted around champion and crusader, while the rest fell somewhere between interested and saboteur. As you can imagine, they were my favorites. It really became a style issue. Why didn't everyone care as much as I did? Why didn't everyone want to win as badly as I did? Why didn't everyone work as hard as I did? For me it was confusing and frustrating. So, I knew I had to change, influence, cajole, and intimidate all of them to make absolutely certain they cared as much as I cared, shared the same obsession with winning I shared and most importantly, worked as hard as I worked! Well, guess what? It reminds me of another story from Buckingham and Coffman's *First, Break All the Rules*.

> There once lived a scorpion and a frog. The scorpion wanted
> to cross the pond, but, being a scorpion, he couldn't swim.
> So he scuttled up to the frog and asked: "Please, Mr. Frog,
> can you carry me across the pond on your back?"
>
> "I would," replied the frog, "but under the circumstances
> I must refuse. You might sting me as I swim across."
>
> "But, why would I do that?" asked the scorpion. "It is not
> in my best interest to do that because you will die, and I will
> drown."
>
> Although the frog knew how lethal scorpions were, the

logic proved quite persuasive. Perhaps, felt the frog, in this one instance the scorpion would keep his tail in check. So the frog agreed. The scorpion climbed onto his back, and together they set off across the pond. Just as they reached the middle of the pond, the scorpion twitched his tail and stung the frog. Mortally wounded, the frog cried out: "Why did you sting me? It is not in your interest to sting me, because now I will die and you will drown."

"I know," replied the scorpion as he sank into the pond. "But, I am a scorpion. I have to sting you. That is my nature."

As I look back on those times, I'm grateful for all of the lessons I took away, none more important than to never take ourselves so seriously that it becomes self-destructive. In the end, in spite of all my attempts at converting our people to being committed like me, I influenced no one. Worse than that, I teetered on the edge of a nervous breakdown. As I watch drug company commercials today describe medication for depression, I now recognize the quiet suffering I was experiencing to the point of becoming totally dysfunctional: chest pains, rapid pulse rate, sweaty palms, sitting in a locked office unable to face all of the problems going on around me. I finally reached out to one of the most important people in my life, Guy Womble.

Guy was our division administrative manager and one of my direct reports. **In his caring and non-threatening way, he helped me realize I was not only doing irreparable damage to myself, but hurting the people I cared about most . . . all because of my obsession with winning.**

Though I don't often discuss my religion, it has always been where I've turned for answers in the most difficult of times. I began attending Mass every day at noon, prayed a lot, and began to read passages from the Bible. I was looking for a way to respond to the obvious mess I had created. When I read from the gospel of the Apostle John, I realized the way in which he wrote scripture was a reflection of his personality. It started to become much clearer to me how this desire to win at all costs had gotten so far out of hand. In John's younger years, he lacked a sense of spiritual equilibrium. His zeal, his intolerance, and his selfish ambition were all sins of imbalance. They were all potential virtues pushed to sinful extremes. That is why the greatest strengths of his character caused his greatest failures. Like the Apostle John, I had turned my greatest strengths into my greatest weakness and the message was quite clear—I had to rebalance my life. As you will read in Truth #10, when that same message was delivered to me in a totally different way, it began both my personal transformation and one I hope has made a difference in other people's lives in a positive way.

Commitment is Not About How a Person Performs, But if They Perform to the Best of Their Ability Every Day for the Rest of Their Lives

If we are not at the high end of the commitment continuum as a champion, crusader, or fanatic (it really is okay to be fanatical) then we will never exploit the style that defines our potential. Being so committed to success/winning, I've made it a habit over the years to observe athletes, salespeople, leaders, parents, and numerous others and have come to the conclusion that high levels of commitment are directly related to courage. The Olympic motto says, "Ask not only for victory, ask for courage. For if you can endure, you bring honor not only to yourself, you bring honor to all of us." Courage is endurance.

Dorothy Bernard said courage is "fear that has said its prayers." George Patton said courage is "fear holding on a minute longer." Plautus said courage is "taking hard knocks when occasion calls." La Rochefoucald said it is "doing without witnesses that which we would be capable of doing before everyone." Dr. Martin Luther King Jr. wrote in one of his letters from the Birmingham jail, "The true measure of a man is not where he stands in time of comfort or convenience but rather where he stands in time of challenge and controversy."

Not being afraid to fail, as I stated in the last chapter, is a precursor to commitment. Once we acknowledge the uncompromised standards of excellence, the only question remaining is how committed we are to the end result. **The relentless pursuit to which we must ultimately commit defines whether we truly are accountable.**

Sterling examples of commitment are plentiful, but I'll share just two. The first is the person I believe is the greatest example of commitment in my lifetime (except for those who have sacrificed their lives for our freedom): Lance Armstrong.

In his book *It's Not About the Bike*, Armstrong shares

extensively his battle with cancer and the courage he demonstrated in beating the disease and winning the grueling Tour de France after chemotherapy. The French press had accused him of doping. When asked about being on a performance-enhancing drug following his first victory (he eventually went on to win an unprecedented seven times), he replied, "The only thing I'm on is my bike busting my ass ten hours a day!"

What Armstrong achieved, in a contest that many sports researchers, coaches, athletes, and fans believe to be the most grueling competitive sports event in the world, is nothing short of a miracle. His commitment to the enormous rigors of his sport is unprecedented.

The second example is more obscure. John Steven Aquari was a long distance runner from Tanzania who competed in the Mexico City Olympics in 1968. During the first mile of the marathon, Aquari fell and badly injured his knee. Hours after the winner had crossed the finish line, the stadium was dark. An ambulance came into the stadium carrying a badly injured runner. Following behind the ambulance was Aquari, stumbling toward the finish line. He fell across it, completing the twenty-six-mile course. When later asked how he could have endured after such a devastating injury, he answered by telling the reporter, "My country didn't send me seven thousand miles to start the race; they sent me seven thousand miles to finish the race."

When we assess whether we are accountable and responsible for what we do every day, the first question we should ask ourselves is, "Can we be trusted?" The second question we must ask ourselves is, "Are we committed to be the best we can be every day, every week, every month, every year for the rest of our lives?"

Every day, ask yourself, "Did I finish the race?"

Discoveries

1 It is reasonable to expect people to embrace commitment but it must be their choice.

2 It takes courage to operate at the high end of the commitment continuum and courage is about endurance—doing without witness what we are capable of doing before everyone.

CHAPTER TEN

Leaders
Stimulate
Loyalty

I'm often asked whether loyalty truly passes the litmus test as the third leg of the stool in defining personal accountability (with trust and commitment serving as the other two). It's a fair question because loyalty is defined much differently today than it was when the journey began and certainly throughout the '90s when we introduced the model within The Berry Company as the operating philosophy. There is strong evidence that mutual disloyalty is not exclusive to employees at work. The lack of loyalty has extended itself far beyond business impacting family, church, school, community, and every aspect of our society. The self-absorption, instant gratification, greed, and winning-at-all-costs mentality that we discussed earlier are both the cause and the effect. So, why continue to embrace loyalty as part of the response to accountability? Simply because I remain firm in my belief that we all want to be part of something bigger than ourselves.

OBSTACLE 9 Lack of Loyalty

Is it the same loyalty that guaranteed lifetime employment that our grandparents and parents believed was their inalienable right? No, it's different but it's also the same. In their book, *The Leadership Challenge*, James M. Kouzes and Barry Z. Posner define this difference when they state:

> In the end, durable relationships are more likely to produce collaboration than short-term ones. But, there is one more important amendment to this. The reality is that people don't stay in one job nor should they. Marriages do fall apart, and abusive ones should end. Companies do fail, sometimes because of bad management and sometimes because the marketplace isn't buying what they are selling. The point is every significant relationship should be treated as if it will last a lifetime and as if it will be important to all parties' mutual success in the future.

I am often amazed at the perception of our MBA students who believe that the majority of CEOs are not unlike Saddam Hussein, Osama Bin Laden, and Kim Jong Il. I always caution them to be careful in their conclusion because I was one of them! Unfortunately, the abuses have been so pervasive over the last several years and continue to be, that we tend to paint all CEOs with the same brush. While the notorious probably represent less than one percent, I do believe far too many

It's Okay to Be Loyal to Your Company, Your Customer, and Your Fellow Employee

CEOs are guilty of paying attention to the wrong investor. They are too concerned about Wall Street, the investment community, the analyst, and the stock price. The investors they need to pay the most attention to are their employees. Employees must commit to something far more meaningful than their money. They invest their heart, soul, blood, and guts each and every day. Commitment is to loyalty what courage is to commitment. Loyalty does not emerge from blind obedience. You can't ask for what you're not willing to give. Loyalty must be more than job security. **As leaders, we've got to give employees a sense of purpose, a set of principles, a vision, a dream, and most importantly, an environment where they can get what they want. Loyalty is much more than unquestionably repeating company spin—you have to believe.**

Frederick F. Reichheld and Thomas Teal, in their book *The Loyalty Effect*, say:

> Loyalty-based management is not just about loyalty to individuals or groups: it's about loyalty to a set of principles that enable a business to serve all of its constituents well through time. Loyalty leaders don't see profits as the primary objective, but as an essential element in the well-being and survival of three principal partners: customers, employees, and investors. Loyalty leaders prefer long-term partnerships. What this means in practice is choosing partners with a healthy respect for human dignity, who will seek and find the elusive balance between self-interest and team interest, partners who want to win but are not willing to win at the team's expense.

I'm confident Reichheld and Teal would find great satisfaction in knowing the behavior-driven model aligns perfectly with this definition of loyalty-based leaders. It's a delicate balance, but when people are given responsibility for results, their commitment grows. I also believe the reverse is just as true. Leave people without responsibility for being accountable for their actions and you will create a hiding place for people who resist change and insist on living in the past. We can't create the future by recreating the past. We also must recognize that we can't create the future without loyal employees, customers, and friends.

Discoveries

1 Loyalty does not emerge from blind obedience. You can't ask for what you're not willing to give.

2 We all want to be part of something bigger than ourselves. Therefore, as leaders we must choose employees with a healthy respect for human dignity and a balance between self-interest and team interest.

CHAPTER ELEVEN

Leaders Encourage Self-Acceptance and Acceptance of Others

The five tenets of the Berry Leadership Pledge directed us to hire good people, give them the tools to do their job, tell them what we expect, share honest feedback, and hold them accountable. The journey is now complete! Oh, I almost forgot. There is one more thing, and it's the most critical part of the message. In Chapter One I described the impact Vince Flowers and Charley Hughes had on my life and ultimately the lives of thousands of others. Convincing me I needed to move from being sales-driven to behavior-driven was, and is, at the heart of this simple (but not easy) approach to performance. While the five tenets define the model, a much deeper understanding of ourselves and each other is necessary if there is any hope of attaining the results we seek. As Paul Harvey so eloquently says, "And now for the rest of the story."

OBSTACLE 10 Externally Imposed Measures

At the conclusion of the week I spent with Vince and Charley in Dallas at the Center for Values Research, they provided me with a very stark assessment of my management style and all of the baggage that went along with it. They said, "While it appears you've been blessed with a wonderful gift to lead, you've got one major problem. You're focused on the wrong thing. You're consumed with external recognition and not internal satisfaction and when you believe that success is determined externally, you open the door to the paralyzing fear of failure. The fallout is even more damaging. Because of your desire to please and impress, you are constantly comparing yourself to others, thus directing your focus on what you can't control."

Wow! You talk about a heavy dose of advice to hear when you're thirty-seven years old. I knew what was coming next. You've got to change! Much to my surprise, Vince and Charley took me down a very different path. They told me I couldn't be anyone other than me and that was okay because it was my assertiveness and competitive personality that got me this far in life. Then, they crystallized it for me! They told me our strengths are our weaknesses. While my passion and intensity are my greatest assets, under pressure they became my greatest liabilities. Instead of using my desire to win as a shoulder for our people to lean on, it had become my sword. **What I perceived to be a major setback professionally and personally had become the most meaningful counsel I had ever received.**

"You've got to learn to accept yourself for who you are because you can't be anybody else," They said. Vince and Charley convinced me that who we are is what makes each of us unique and you can't, nor do you want to, change who you are. They persuaded me that my competitiveness and intensity manifested into passion that ultimately defined my uniqueness. And this is nothing more than an extension of love: love for self, for others, and for what you do every day. Finally, they told me this self-awareness will ultimately define my career, as well as my life.

Accept Yourself
as You Exist

We've often heard phrases along the lines of . . .

"To thine own self be true. Thou shalt not be false to any other man."

"If it's going to be, it's up to me."

"The less I am of you, the more I am of me."

Serving as executive director of the Center for Leadership & Executive Development at the University of Dayton has afforded me the opportunity to be exposed to the world's thought leaders on the topic of leadership. They have validated what we learned "at the edge of the cliff" in Buffalo. As I searched for confirmation, I uncovered numerous references but nothing resonated until I came across the last chapter in Kouzes and Posner's *The Leadership Challenge*. The leadership lesson they describe is one they value as the secret to life. In studying leadership's best, they ask U.S. Army Major General John H. Stanford how he went about developing leaders in the many leadership roles he had the privilege of holding in his career. He described the following:

> When anyone asks me that question, I tell them I have the secret to success in life. The secret to success is to stay in love. Staying in love gives you the fire to ignite other people, to see inside other people, to have a greater desire to get things done than other people. A person who is not in love doesn't really feel the kind of excitement that helps them to get ahead and to lead others to achieve. I don't know any other fire, any other thing in life that is more exhilarating and is more positive a feeling than love is.

The authors go on to say that of all the things sustaining a leader over time, love is the most lasting. **Leadership is not an affair with the head. Leadership is an affair with the heart.**

I'm convinced the affair starts with accepting ourselves. One of the many reasons I spend so much time at the University of Dayton is I believe the Marianist-influenced mission of "Learn, Lead, and Serve" truly gets at the heart of leadership. That is, we can never be a leader until we are a servant. I became very interested in servant leadership a couple of years before I retired because I recognized it filled in some of the blanks for me. I borrowed a number of books from John Geiger, the former university provost, to better understand what makes servant leadership so crucial in effectively leading others.

Robert K. Greenleaf, essayist and the father of servant leadership, draws a distinction between natural leaders and natural servants. Natural leaders are decisive and need to be in charge. Natural servants will assume leadership only if they define it as a way to serve. Greenleaf explains that while most people believe natural leaders use a more directive style and natural servants use a more participative style, this is not the case. He says this belief is inaccurate because it confuses style with character. Natural servants will use whatever leadership style is necessary to best serve the needs of those they lead. **It also should be noted that the biblical image of servant leadership is**

163

that of the shepherd, because the flock is not there for the sake of the shepherd; the shepherd is there for the sake of the flock.

Another lesson from Greenleaf is that too often we look outside of ourselves for answers. That search is simply a reflection of our own belief of not having enough, not being enough, not doing enough. **The answers always reside inside of us. We simply must be willing to accept the truth. It's the willingness to accept ourselves as we exist.**

There is a wonderful book titled *I'm Dysfunctional, You're Dysfunctional*, by Wendy Kaminer. The book focuses on the issue of co-dependency. Kaminer talks about self-love as a key ingredient. This points out that if we don't love ourselves first, we depend on others for our own personal happiness.

Self-love is a contemporary term, but nearly one hundred and fifty years ago, one of our greatest leaders recognized the principle. When asked about the success of his presidency, given the enormous difficulties, Abraham Lincoln said, "If I only have one friend when I leave this office, and that friend resides inside of me, I will have been successful."

Acceptance of yourself has to start with each of us individually as leaders, peers, parents and friends. We must trust that our beliefs are our own. The longer we wait to find our own voice, the less chance we have of finding it. I'm so grateful I was able to find my voice in 1981. In the end, at least for me, it comes down to faith.

Consider this beautiful poem:

> Doubt sees the obstacles, faith sees the way,
>
> Doubt sees the dark of night, faith sees the day,
>
> Doubt dares to take a step, faith soars on high,
>
> Doubt asks the question "who believes?" and faith answers "I"

For me, it's about faith in God, and faith in who I am. Once I discovered and accepted myself, I recognized my faith was not belief without proof, but rather trust without reservation. **Learning to accept myself** allowed me to trust my instincts and devote myself fully to others without the need for that external acceptance which held me hostage for the first thirty-seven years of my life. It is important to recognize that as leaders, it doesn't lessen the burden of responsibility. **Once we learn to accept ourselves, we are void of self-doubt. With that peace of mind, we are free to extend our energy outward to others.**

The first example I can provide is a story about our oldest son, Peter. In 1992, he wrote an essay for admission to the University of Notre Dame that required him to describe a childhood experience that influenced his young adult life:

> It was May of 1988 and I was a freshman at Alter High
> School in Kettering, Ohio. I was 4' 10" and weighed 85
> pounds and three years earlier it was discovered that I was

suffering from a hormone deficiency that would deny me of my natural growth potential. I was on the drug Protrupin 7 and gave myself hormone shots three days a week. Even though I was competitive academically, because of my size, I was the brunt of everyone's jokes. I had been cut in basketball and had no self-esteem. I was a very unhappy child.

It's now December of 1992 and I am a senior at John Carroll Catholic in Birmingham, Alabama. I am 5' 8", I weigh 150 pounds, have a 4.3 GPA and I'm fourth in my class. I'm President of the National Honor Society, President of the Concert Choir, and 7 time member of first honors. I tutor Spanish three days a week. I'm an Ambassador for Life and recruit in Catholic grade schools. I'm a three-year letterman in baseball and a two-year letterman in basketball.

What happened to me between then and now was my parents were transferred to Birmingham and asked me if I wanted to repeat my freshman year; I jumped at the chance and have never looked back.

What I learned between then and now is that self-esteem in not about size, intelligence, or athletic ability, but rather it's about confidence and as I look forward to the rest of my life, I no longer fear the outcome but look forward to the challenge.

Peter, a physician, graduated from the University of Notre Dame and the University of South Alabama College of Medicine.

The second example is about our second son, Matthew. Different from his brother, and as parents we all know they are special gifts of God, he matured much later. After graduating from the University of Dayton (at least one of my sons saw the light and followed in his father's footsteps), Matt eventually joined The Berry Company as a sales representative. It was during those years of both success and enormous pressure of being the son of the CEO that Matt came to both his mother and I and asked for help.

He had come to the harsh realization that he was an alcoholic, that he had a chronic, progressive, and potentially fatal disease and, most of all, he needed our help. Like all caring parents, we gave Matt our unconditional love and support. As Matt so passionately says:

> In no way do I view this experience negatively. The hard part for me was admitting I had a problem and coming to grips with the changes I had to make in my life. None of these are bad things.
>
> I thought they were at first but because of the process of getting and staying sober, I have been exposed to a lifestyle

and way of life—or my spirituality if you will—that I would have never have known. I have learned what it means to love people unconditionally, to love my God unconditionally, and most importantly to love myself.

For the first time in my life, I know who I am, who I really am, and I know my happiness is my journey not my destination. As I heard it so eloquently once before, "I may not have gone where I intended to go, but I think I ended up where I needed to be."

I'm proud to say that Matt has been sober now for three years and devotes a significant part of his life helping young people recognize that alcohol and drugs are not the solution to self-worth. (We teach the Life Skills course at UD together, which is one of the coolest things we've ever done as father and son.) Watching Matt grow from a young man who was looking for answers outside himself to someone who will devote his life to helping others is the second example of what I believe truly happens when we learn to accept ourselves.

Accept Yourself as You Exist

•

Accept Others as They Exist

As Truth #10 unfolds, **once we've learned to accept ourselves as we exist, then and only then, can we learn to accept others as they exist.** This is where the magic starts. This is where the model begins to take shape.

The opposite of acceptance is rejection. I marvel at how young couples fall in love because they admire the qualities in each other and spend the rest of their lives trying to change each other. Parents bring a beautiful child into this world and then rob them of their right to find their own identity because the parents are living their lives vicariously through their children. Even at The Berry Company, in spite of our sophisticated assessment tools, on occasion, we still tried to change people.

Ignorance is the enemy of love. **When we deepen our level of understanding of others, we no longer fear the differences, but rather we learn to honor them.** It's the power of two, times four, times sixteen, times thirty-two, etc. It's about the power of relationships. Buckingham and Coffman address this by disputing "The Golden Rule." Remember the Golden Rule? "Treat people as you would like to be treated." Their research finds that the best managers break The Golden Rule every day. Instead, they say, don't treat people like you want to be treated, but rather

treat each person as he or she would like to be treated, bearing in mind who he or she is.

We introduced situational leadership to The Berry Company in 1986 and it is still part of the management philosophy. The key to the program is recognizing an individual's development needs and then providing training to support improvement in specific areas. The Value Systems model, developed by psychologist Dr. Clare W. Graves, recognizes at what value system each individual is functioning and managing the relationship at that level.

While there has been so much written and published about leadership, the fact is, all the models, philosophies and approaches are ineffective without genuine care, concern, and love for the individual. Without love, those approaches and the many others being hailed as the answer are doomed to failure.

In Chapter Three we reflected upon those people who were the greatest inspiration in our lives. By definition, we were not inspired by the people who tried to convince us to be somebody else. Quite the contrary, those who inspired us were the people who convinced us that we could be more than we were, took us to places we never thought we could go, and believed in us more than we believed in ourselves. They loved us!

In the early '80s at The Berry Company, we introduced an assessment tool that was developed in collaboration with DDI (Development Dimensions International) out of Pittsburgh and it did a wonderful job of identifying specific behaviors needed to lead and manage our sales force. Being a sales organization, the majority of first level managers rise from the ranks of the sales force and, as you can imagine, they possess all of the necessary qualities including passion, commitment, and competitiveness. During Berry Leadership Training, I shared two experiences new managers would encounter during their first six months; how they would handle these situations would help them define whether management was where they truly belonged. First, they would have to deal with the lack of recognition and second, the personal frustration of not accepting others for whom they were. Without exception, the managers all struggled with both.

After that experience, I encouraged them to be mindful of two powerful lessons. First, help every individual you supervise to be more than they can be...and not something they're not. Secondly, each and every day, strive to make a difference in someone's life. Take that responsibility seriously and recognize that being in a position of leadership is a gift and a blessing.

Upon retirement, I was fortunate to have a number of recognition events in my honor. As I reflected on the many wonderful things that were said and written, there was not one reference to the number of quotas made or missed, the number of times we made our net income, and only a few references to our many contract acquisitions during those last nine years.

Since retirement, I have had the privilege of maintaining contact with a number of our employees. There has never been mention of quotas made or missed, the number of times we made our net income, and only a few references to our many contract acquisitions! Every memory, reflection, or gesture of thanks has to do with the fact that in some small way, I made a difference in their lives. **In the end, that's how all of our lives are judged.**

I have a priest friend who has administered last rites on hundreds of occasions. He will be quick to tell you that in sharing those last moments of life, no one has ever expressed regret about not making enough quotas or spending more time at work. They talk about wishing they would have cared more, loved more and gave more. It's a sobering thought, but one we all need to address now, not when it's too late!

In the final analysis, there is nothing more important than being important to someone. I've heard it said **"to the whole world we may be one person, but to one person we could be the whole world."**

I've avoided discussing my involvement in a number of community activities previously, but it's appropriate to mention here. As current Chair of the United Way Board for our three counties and campaign chair in 2003, I have visited over sixty-five agencies that are part of the United Way network. During these trips, I witnessed true hopelessness for the first time in my life. Not hopelessness in terms of a terminal illness, which some of us have unfortunately dealt with, but rather hopelessness from pure, utter despair by people who were either born into a circumstance or have fallen upon hard times and have little chance of getting out.

Along the way, I've met amazing people who perform tiny miracles every day because they take the time to care. I'm convinced every problem in this world can be solved if someone cares enough. The lesson here is simple and straightforward. Corporations do not fail or succeed because of the economy, competition, or emerging technology. They fail because of their inability to care. Their inability to respond is purely the result of the lack of focused energy inside their four walls as a result of not accepting each other and the God-given talent we all bring to relationships. **It's really simple, it's just not easy!**

Here are a couple of examples of what happens when we do take the time to care.

One morning when I stopped at a local convenient mart to get a cup of coffee, a gentleman came up and asked me if I was Pete Luongo. When I responded yes, he told me he was Eddie Clemons and that he wrestled for me thirty years earlier at Carroll High School. We exchanged pleasantries and Ed then confided in me that I was right and he shouldn't have quit wrestling his senior year for that girl. I told Ed it was a little late for redemption and he was doing just fine.

Several weeks went by, and as fate would have it, I ran into Ed again. He asked me if I would come over and watch his sons Tommy and Jeff wrestle. I said yes and later walked into that gym for the first time in twenty years. After the match, Ed brought his two sons over to meet me. I can't tell you how proud Ed was to introduce his sons to his high school wrestling coach. I'll never forget walking out of the gym that night and feeling like a million dollars. Thirty years later and I made a small difference in someone's life.

The second story happened the first year I was teaching Strategy in the MBA program at the University of Dayton. There was a student, Richard Fulwiler, who sat on the left side of the room. Richard is handicapped in that he does not have full use of his right arm and he has a slight speech impediment. Nonetheless, Richard is very bright and was very active in class.

One evening after class, he approached Dick Flaute, another executive-in-residence, and I in regards to getting some tips on interviewing since he had just lost his job when his company moved his job overseas.

During the course of that meeting, Richard told me he had suffered a massive stroke at the age of 12, twelve years prior, which had paralyzed his entire left side. I was absolutely shocked that in just a dozen years, Richard had made such a remarkable recovery. I told Richard the only tip I could give him was that the next time he went on a job interview, he should tell the interviewer his story. As I told Richard, if you tell the miracle you've accomplished in just twelve years, they'll hire you. More importantly, I told Richard people will accept him for who he is because he truly is an amazing young man.

As part of Richard's remarkable recovery, as he described

it, "I have undergone many challenges since that day in 1989. Everything from the length of time it took me to write or take tests, to the numbers of peas that may have tremored off my spoon, to the jeers and jokes made by others, to having to ask my state representative to make it so I could get my driver's license when the license bureau said no. Ironically, though, my mind, the culprit of the stroke and ultimately all these challenges was also the source of inspiration and power to overcome all the many challenges I have faced."

Within two weeks, he was hired at The Berry Company (I still have some influence). Richard, now married, is at LexisNexis as a project manager and doing extremely well, both professionally and personally.

As a sequel to this story, and not long after, I was in a nearby clothing store when a man introduced himself to me and told me he was Richard's neighbor. He told me what a huge difference I made in Richard's life by giving him so much encouragement about how special he was. It's amazing what a difference just thirty minutes of our lives can make when we just take the time to care.

Accept Yourself as You Exist

•

Accept Others as They Exist

•

In the Context of Differences and Similarities, Find Better Ways of Coping Effectively as a Behavior-Driven Organization

Great sports dynasties call it chemistry. Great corporations call it culture. Great relationships simply call it love. How do you know when you have it? What does it look like, and how do you describe it?

We all know when it's there and we know when it's not. When asked the question, "Are you proud to work for The Berry Company?" the employee responses were consistently positive between 95 and 98% of the time.

When I asked the employees why they felt that way, regardless of whether it was Anchorage, Alaska, Birmingham, Alabama, or Rochester, New York, the response was always the same: it was our culture that made them proud to work at Berry.

One of my priorities before I retired was to provide the next generation of leadership with an understanding of what that really meant. I mentioned earlier in the book that we engaged Don Blohowiak from the Lead Well Institute to help us better understand our culture. After extensive work with our employees, his findings articulated the six attributes that he believed placed The Berry Company in the same breath as The Marine Corps and Southwest Airlines, companies which he holds up as gold standard.

The six attributes of Berry's culture were:

- Results Count, but People Count More

- A Great Place to Work: Structured Support for High

Expectations

- Quality Product Made Special for both the Employees and the Customers

- Support for Individual Achievement: A Focus on Personal Growth

- Sustained Success through Employee Longevity

- A Business with More than a Touch of Humanity

While these key cultural attributes provided us with a much deeper understanding of what made The Berry Company special, it also validated the impact "The Leadership Pledge" had on our ability to execute.

Recruit, Hire, and Retain

Provide the Support

Set the Standard

Share Honest Feedback

Encourage Individual Accountability

Overlaying the two, you can see how they fit together perfectly.

Recruit, Hire, and Retain

Results Count, but People Count More

Provide the Support

A Great Place to Work: Structured Support for High Expectations

Set the Standard

Quality Product Made Special for both the Employees and the Customers

Share Honest Feedback

Support for Individual Achievement: A Focus on Personal Growth

Encourage Individual Accountability

Sustained Success through Employee Longevity

Finally, when I linked A Business With More Than A Touch of Humanity with "Love for ourselves, love for each other, and love for what we do everyday," I was satisfied that we had created a code of conduct that provided structure, discipline, and a set of behaviors that drives sustainable results while allowing our employees to feel valued, respected, and part of something special.

When I left Buffalo in 1984, we had a sign in our lobby reading "inside these four walls only exist solutions." We only had one rule: If anyone had a frown on their face, any one of our 107 employees was encouraged to ask what we could do to help you feel better.

Earlier in the book, I talked about "getting to the mountain" only six times in sixty-three years and I want to share a second experience as I bring the book to a close. It happened in 1984. It was two years before divestiture and AT&T was still responsible for canvass reviews. The canvass review team was made of members from other yellow page sales organizations throughout the Bell System and their role was to evaluate all functions of your canvass from operating procedures to sales effectiveness and everything in between.

These reviews were incredibly stressful and in some extreme cases, could be career threatening. Even though we were in the second year of this business transformation and I was confident we were moving in a positive direction, I viewed this as the first true test of our progress.

The report that followed the review cited the Buffalo canvass as ranking in the top three of all reviews conducted throughout the United States. What an incredible feeling it was for our entire division, not to mention the personal satisfaction and vindication I felt during that moment. It convinced me that while there was still much to be done, I was on the right track in pursuing the model that was grounded in love for each other, ourselves, and what we do every day.

The Leadership Pledge

In all things—
Behavior Drives Results

- **Recruit, Hire, and Retain**
- **Provide the Support**
- **Set the Standard**
- **Share Honest Feedback**
- **Encourage Individual Accountability**

This book's title, *10 Truths About Leadership* is all wrapped up in "The Leadership Pledge." To the same end, "The Leadership Pledge" is on display in all the Berry offices where I hope it will remain as a reminder to everyone there and the readers of this book that behavior truly does drive results!

Discoveries

1 When we believe success is determined externally, we open ourselves up to the power of failure and focus on what we can't control. Once you have learned to accept yourself, you are void of self-doubt and with that peace of mind you are able to extend yourself to others.

2 When you deepen your level of understanding of others, you learn to honor your differences, not fear them. Then and only then can you help others become more than they can be.

3 When organizations focus on the behavior that drives results and possess a collective resolve built on self-acceptance and acceptance of others, results will follow.

CHAPTER TWELVE

Final Thoughts

When I retired as president/CEO of The Berry Company, I made the decision to devote the rest of my life to giving back. My focus was on health and human services, economic development, and education. I'm thankful I can do this across a number of organizations, including working as board chair of our three-county United Way agency, serving as board chair of a large hospital, and participating on the executive committee of the Dayton Development Coalition, which is comprised of thirty-six CEOs focused on economic development for our region.

My focus on education comes to light at the University of Dayton where I teach leadership to undergraduate and graduate students, as executive director of the University's Center for Leadership & Executive Develop-ment, and on the University's Board of Trustees, and as a chair on the athletics board.

I mention these because, throughout the book, references have been made to all of these initiatives. Through these experiences, I have come to realize so many of us are so immersed in our professional lives that it hinders our best intentions to give back to our communities in different and meaningful ways.

Whether visiting the sixty-four agencies our United Way

group supported in 2003, becoming intimately engaged in a system merger for our hospital, teaching Leadership in the classroom, speaking to over one hundred different organizations, or serving as the Executive Director of the University of Dayton's Center for Leadership & Executive Development . . . all these things have provided me with very unique perspectives.

I've witnessed hopelessness for the first time, been exposed to industries in health care, education and the defense sector, and have been privileged to speak at Dr. Martin Luther King Jr. celebrations. I could fill up another chapter on these and so many more meaningful and life-altering experiences.

All of these experiences have confirmed my belief that our society is so focused on winning that this obsession negatively influences all phases of our lives, from our professional careers to parenthood and everything in between. Its manifestations include greed, self-indulgence, instant gratification, and winning at all costs.

Is the pursuit of success and winning really a bad thing? There is a groundswell today purporting that more important than winning, is the need to serve a higher purpose. The ultimate challenge for all of us as individuals, regardless of whether we're bosses, employees, coaches, parents, teachers or students, is to never commit the sin of selfishness, ingratitude or ungratefulness as we pursue our dreams. I believe the only time we realize our dreams is when we help others realize their dreams.

When we help people get in the right circumstances to maximize their God-given talent, provide them whatever tools and support they need to be successful, make certain there is a clear understanding of expectations, share with them honest and open feedback, and finally allow them to be accountable and responsible for their own destiny . . . only then will we have mastered the model.

Ralph Waldo Emerson wrote so beautifully when he said:

> To laugh often and love much, to win the respect of intelligent people, to earn the approbation of honest critics, and endure the betrayal of false friends, to appreciate beauty, to find the best in others, and to give of oneself; to leave the world a better place whether by a healthy child, a redeemed social condition, or a garden patch . . . to have lived your life with enthusiasm and to have sung with exaltation, and finally to know that one life has breathed a little easier because you have lived, that is to have been successful.

It's the magic of all relationships, and if we use these truths as a constant reminder of how to successfully manage relationships, we will achieve the ultimate goal of life by making a difference and create an environment where employees feel valued, respected and part of something special.

About the Author

Pete Luongo retired as President and CEO of the The Berry Company in August of 2003, a career that spanned more than thirty-three years. During his last nine years, he was part of the team that led the billion-and-a-half dollar yellow page advertising agency through a period of record sales growth, numerous contract acquisitions, and the perpetuation of the nearly one-hundred-year-old company as an industry leader as well as "a great place to work."

While his goal of giving back has encompassed many pursuits, none is more important than taking his **10 Truths About Leadership** to organizations throughout the world. An accomplished business leader, corporate strategist and compelling communicator, his message transcends business transformation, emerging technology, product innovation, and strategic imperatives.

Let the "10 Truths" benefit your organization!

Everyone wants to feel valued, respected, and part of something special. Organizations that balance personnel and financial goals create exceptional employee allegiance as well as record-setting achievements. Pete Luongo, by virtue of his decades of corporate success and developmental work with small and mid-sized companies through regional coalitions and advisory boards, can help your company turn around troubling situations and drive positive results. Pete's presentation will help you and your staff focus on behavior as the principles to operational success.

To bring Pete Luongo to your organization, go to **www.petespeaks.com.**